THE MASTERFUL WRITING
COLLECTION

*Comprising the Dunlith Hill Writing Guides
to Story Theory, Verisimilitude, and
Character and Archetype*

DEREN HANSEN

Dunlith Hill

CONTENTS

INTRODUCTION

In order to master the craft of writing and the art of storytelling you must internalize the rhythms of the human experience and the ways we share that experience. There are deep and consistent patterns in the ways we tell stories, weave narrative illusions, and develop fascinating characters.

This collection includes three Dunlith Hill Writers Guides:

Story Theory: How to Write Like J.R.R. Tolkien in Three Easy Steps

Verisimilitude: How Illusions, Confidence Games, and Skillful Lying can Improve Your Fiction

Character and Archetype: How to Make Readers Fall in Love with your Imaginary Friends

When you understand and apply the simple but powerful patterns taught in these guides, you will be well on your way to becoming a masterful writer.

PART I.

STORY THEORY

CHAPTER 1.

WHY DO WE TELL STORIES?

Watching an ant hill, it's hard not to marvel at the way in which they work together. The magic, according to entomologists, is a matter of chemistry. Ants exchange chemical signals when they meet, enabling them to recognize members of their colony and coordinate activities.

Storytelling is our version of chemical signaling. Long before we worked out conventions for courses, text books, encyclopedias, etc., we told stories to convey information and coordinate activities. Stories are the original, "how-to." They say, in essence, "If you find yourself in a situation like this, here's how to deal with it."

STORIES ARE ABOUT CAUSE AND EFFECT

Ernest Hemingway once won a bar bet that he could write a story in only six words. His words were:

"For sale: baby shoes. Never used."

Like other bar bets, it's impressive, but not quite what it appears to be. In particular, Hemingway's story isn't a story, it's a story prompt.

In arguing that Hemingway did indeed have a story, you might point out how each two-word phrase is like one of three acts, taking us in a different and more dramatic direction at each turn. That's true, but I have yet to meet anyone who isn't intrigued by those six words: they can't help speculating and filling in details to create a story in their own mind. And the story is always about what caused the effect of someone possessing unused baby shoes.

J. Michael Straczynski explains story this way:

- The king died and then the queen died. (Not a story)
- The queen died because the king died. (A story)

In the first case, we simply have two events—two royal deaths listed in the chronicles. In the second, the story organizes the two events into a cause/effect relationship. Naturally, there's a great deal more to a satisfying story—a novel, for example, will describe many causes and effects on different levels and in different dimensions.

Must all stories show cause and effect? What about literary fiction?

Don't be misled by the siren song of the literati and their conceit that a nuanced character study is superior to plot-driven commercial offerings. Even a character study is about the causes and effects of the character's beliefs and behaviors.

STORIES ATTRIBUTE SIGNIFICANCE

There is a Native American tale which explains how the mountains surrounding the tribal homeland were created when the trickster trapped giants and turned them to stone as punishment for their wickedness. Similarly, one of the remarkable things about **The Lord of the Rings** is the way in which Tolkien produced a fictional landscape full of the significance accumulated over the course of three ages: there were stories, often only hinted at in the text, behind so much of the landscape that it became a character in its own right. In both cases, it is the stories that give the landscape significance.

Stories work their magic on people and events as well as physical features. They tell, and more importantly show, why we should care about someone or something. By rehearsing the cause of a particular effect, they teach us why the subject is important and stands out from others like it.

Wits have wryly observed that we can't collectively understand a tragedy until we've watched the made-for-television movie about it. If we peel away the cynicism, the remaining kernel of truth is that by defining meaning and attributing significance, stories are how we make sense of the confusing world in which we live.

STORY PROBLEMS ARE NON-TRIVIAL

There is an eternal law, inscribed into the very foundation of the universe before even gods appeared, that any home improvement project will require at least three trips to the store.

Don't believe me?

Consider the archetypical home improvement project:

1. Having decided to undertake some repair or improvement, you go to the store and get what you need.
2. After working on the project for a while, you make another trip to the store to get all the things you didn't know you needed.
3. Finally, a few injuries and expletives later, you make a final trip to the store to get what you really need (as well as to replace the pieces you broke).

Of course, there are many times when you make one trip because you know what you're doing and what you need. But you don't tell a story about those episodes because a *this-was-the-problem-so-I-got-the-part-I-needed-and-fixed-it* story is boring—in fact, it's not a story, it's a recipe.

For a story to be interesting, it must show how the protagonist triangulated on a solution to a difficult problem. Each try is a possible solution and each fail shows why the solution falls short, as well as ratcheting up the scope of the problem. In the realm of DIY, for example, you may fail to reattach the loose tile in the bathroom because the wallboard behind has water damage, but you can't just replace the wallboard because the pipe inside is leaking.

And suddenly, without trying, we've stumbled upon the three-act story structure:

• Act 1 is an attempt to solve the story problem that fails.

- Act 2 is another attempt to solve the story problem that also fails.

- Act 3 is the attempt to solve the story problem that finally succeeds.

If you scrape away all the formal baggage around *The Three Act Structure* it really is that simple.

THE BEST STORIES ARE EDGY

We often hear agents and editors want stories that are *edgy, push the envelope,* and talk about how things *really* are.

The edge in question is usually the edge of social acceptability, where the scent of the forbidden entices our voyeuristic impulses. From a business perspective (and without trying to sound too cynical), it's also much easier to sell something offering readers a chance to step vicariously outside common social constraints.

The topic can easily become contentious. There are readers who feel life is too short to waste on vanilla when there are more exotic flavors to be had on the edge. Others hear, "edgy," and immediately think, "uncomfortable," "gratuitous," or even, "marketing gimmick."

It's unfortunate that there's a fair amount of ammunition for readers who associate *edgy* with *gimmicky* because there's an important place in the grand conversation for stories about the edges—not of acceptability but of society.

Stories from the social periphery give voice to people and experiences that are minimized or ignored. Going to the edge is certainly important for social justice, but it's even more important as a source of variability and vitality. Chaos theory, for example, shows that the dynamic equilibrium between order and chaos is the region where the most interesting and complex things happen. Another way to think of it is that the tendency of society to move toward monoculture is offset by the variations and novelties that arise on its periphery.

But there's an even deeper point: at a structural level, the best stories are always edgy in the sense that they take the protagonist out to the edge of their known world and then beyond. Whether the journey is actual or emotional, it's only in the unmediated wild, beyond the edge of the safe and comfortable, where character is revealed and proven.

$$* * *$$

This book focuses on the structural underpinnings of a sustained narrative. In an effort to express ideas clearly and succinctly, some of what follows may seem a bit academic.

Don't be put off by the tone.

The concepts we'll explore are simple, but have profound implications for stories and storytelling. If you can master the patterns, you'll open up rich new dimensions in your writing

We begin, in chapter two, with a look at the way in which stories are models—like maps, they emphasize some details and suppress others. Many of the rules about which writers agonize are simply heuristics for creating satisfying narrative models. But models are patterns, not recipes—something we make clear in chapter three.

Chapter four explores the recurring pattern of threes in many kinds of cultural expressions, including storytelling, and argues three acts, parts, or beats in a story correspond to the minimum container of significance. How do you go from the simplicity of a beginning, middle, and end to the narrative complexity of a satisfying novel? Chapter five provides the fractal answer in three easy steps. In chapter six, we turn from structure to dynamics with a look at story drivers. The discussion continues in chapter seven, where we focus on the kind of conflict that advances a story. Drawing upon all we've covered, in chapter eight we explore the art of the long form: beyond the principles of good storytelling we've covered in the earlier part of the book, what do you need to keep readers engaged for hundreds of pages? Finally, in chapter nine, we close with a look at the practical skills of editing and revising that you'll need to transform your application of story theory into something someone else might actually want to read.

CHAPTER 2.

STORIES ARE MODELS

Models are selective representations of something else: they emphasize some aspects of the subject and suppress others. A model that matches every aspect of its subject perfectly is a copy.

Why would we prefer the imperfect subset of a model over the full fidelity of the real thing? The purpose of a model is to make some aspect of the subject clearer than it might be in reality.

Brandon Sanderson said, "Fantasy is like an experiment: human characters are the control, and the fantastic (world) is the experiment." That is, speculative fiction—at least those stories in which the fantastic setting isn't simply stage dressing—is an imperfect model of reality. We use the license to extend or alter reality afforded by fantasy to make the human subjects or themes of the story clearer.

Storytelling is a richer, more visceral model than, say, a chart or graph because readers experience the story as it unfolds. For example, writing in the Harvard Business Review, Warren G. Bennis and James O'Toole cite the example of a Stanford business course taught, in part, with novels:

> "When the hard-nosed behavioral scientist James March taught his famous course at Stanford using War and Peace and other novels as texts, he emphatically was not teaching a literature course. He was drawing on works of imaginative literature to exemplify the behavior of people in business organizations in a way that was richer and more realistic than any journal article or textbook." [1]

Speculative fiction, however, doesn't have a monopoly on fictional model-making. All stories are selective narratives. And it is that selectivity which makes stories better than life. We don't want to hear about all the ordinary, boring things that happened between the interesting parts. Imagine how tedious a narrative would be if we had to slog through everything the characters did and thought during their waking hours. Instead, we want to hear the heroes realize they can cut the bad guy off at the pass, skip the twelve tedious hours it took to actually get to the pass, and get on with the showdown.

THE RULE OF TWO

Readers, whether by intuition or training, understand stories are models. This is why, at least initially, they are willing to treat everything the author presents as potentially significant, keeping track of details in anticipation of a reward from the author for their attention.

You've probably heard this principle expressed in terms of, "Chekov's gun." According to Wikipedia, "Chekhov's gun is the literary technique whereby an element is introduced early in the story, but its significance does not become clear until later on." [2]

Think of this as a species of foreshadowing. Students of literature, especially ones who aspire to write, can work themselves into a tizzy trying to find or create foreshadowing. At a structural level, however, the idea, which I call, "The Rule of Two," is simple: anything to which you call attention in your story must appear at least twice.

Many middle-grade stories, for example, open with bullies oppressing the protagonist. Then something wonderful happens, the hero goes off to a magical world, and we never hear another peep from the bully. Structurally, the author is telling us the bullies are irrelevant to the larger story—which leaves readers wondering why they had to hear about them in the first place. If, on the other hand, you bring the bully back into the story a second time—if only to show the main character has changed enough that his or her old nemesis is irrelevant—you elevate the bully from set dressing to part of the story.

This is a simple rule, so don't over-think it.

Don't, for example, try to work everything you mention during the course of the novel in to the climax and dénouement. The second appearance of something that comes up in the beginning can be later in the beginning or the middle just as well as the end.

Writers who use throwaways—elements that appear only once—squander readers' efforts to pay attention and risk losing their good will. This, of course, doesn't mean everything in a story must have deeper significance—sometimes a waiter is simply a waiter.

Rather, you need to take care that you're not signaling readers to pay more attention to something than it deserves.

If you think of your story as a model it's easier to see how over-emphasizing elements that are subsidiary to the main story can distract and confuse readers.

POSITIVE AND NEGATIVE SPACE

The way in which selective emphasis creates rhythm and movement in your stories is exemplified by the architectural concepts of positive and negative spaces. In his book, **101 Things I Learned in Architecture School**, Matthew Frederick gives this definition:

> "Positive spaces are almost always preferred by people for lingering and social interaction. Negative spaces tend to promote movement rather than dwelling in place." [3]

In narrative, showing is a dwelling space, telling is a pass-through space—conceptually, we move though the telling and linger in the showing. The pass-through spaces of action and the dwelling spaces of quieter segments give us temporal rhythm. Tension moves us through negative emotional space into the release of a positive dwelling space. In all narrative dimensions the mix of positive and negative—dwelling and pass-through—spaces creates a hierarchy of meaning.

As in art, so too in life.

We live a fair portion of our day in pass-through spaces, taking care of one thing and then moving on to another. Time and space to dwell, thinking slow thoughts or simply being still, are rare. Indeed, the dawning world of pervasive interconnectivity seems driven by forces determined to never leave us alone with our thoughts. But dwelling spaces are where new thoughts are born and where muses nurture the tender shoots of newly sprouted stories. You'll find it difficult to weave an artful mix of positive and negative narrative spaces in your stories if your own life is bereft of one or the other.

NARRATIVE MODE

The narrator creates the skeleton of your narrative model. Your choice of narrative mode and perspective constrains what can and cannot be included in your story model.

Your narrative mode depends on the grammatical person—first, second, or third: I, you, or he and she—in which you tell your story and whether it has one or more narrators.

- **First Person (I)**—feels intimate because you are in your main character's head and can show their thoughts. While you can only show the action the narrator sees, it is the easiest narrative mode to master because it is the way in which most people tell stories.

- **Second Person (You)**—is currently used primarily for instructional or didactic writing (e.g., this book). It is rarely used in fiction outside of choose-your-own-ending books. It is difficult to make second person sound natural to modern readers.

- **Third Person (He/She)**—has been the most common narrative mode for centuries, which means readers assume it's the natural way to write stories. It's also quite flexible: you can stay very close to your main character, listening to their thoughts, and achieving nearly the same degree of intimacy as first person, or you can zoom out, switching among characters, following the action, and giving readers more information than any single character possesses. But that flexibility means it's much easier to make mistakes that leave readers confused about narrators and who knows what.

NARRATIVE PERSPECTIVE

Narrative perspective is a combination of the choice of the point (or points) of view from which the story will be told and the degree of intimacy readers will have with the narrator.

POINT OF VIEW

Choosing the character from whose point-of-view the story will be told is an art that depends on the nature of the story you wish to tell. We can't do justice to the topic here, but a good rule of thumb is to use the character that has the most to lose.

You may be tempted to have multiple narrators if at different points in the story different characters have more to lose. Or you may want multiple narrators to show more action and reveal more information than any single character could see or do. Whatever the reason, you make the task of telling your story more difficult with each additional narrator because you must take extra care to make sure readers know who is telling the story. In general, this means you should only switch the point-of-view at a scene or chapter break.

Another subtle challenge with multiple points of view is that it's easy to avoid going deep enough into any one character to reveal something meaningful about them. Switching the narrator is like switching tasks at work: readers must file everything they know about one character and then open a new folder and reacquaint themselves with a different character. Clearly, readers can keep track of a few characters, but as you divide their attention among points of view they'll feel less attached to any one character.

NARRATIVE INTIMACY

The spectrum of intimacy ranges from a telepathic tap, through which we're privy to the narrator's subjective thoughts and feelings, to a journalistic or cinematic mode, where we observe the characters objectively and can only infer what's going on in their heads from their actions.

There's also a special perspective: the omniscient narrator or the author's point-of-view, which has access to every character's thoughts and feelings. It may seem like a clever way to have both intimacy and scope, but it is difficult to carry off this narrative mode without undermining the story by leaving readers feeling too detached.

First person gives us definitional intimacy because it is now synonymous with stream of thought: we assume we're in the character's head, privy to all their thoughts. It wasn't always this way. There's an earlier tradition where first person implied a statement by an eye-witness. **Treasure Island** is a first person narrative, but we never hear Jim Hawkins wondering whether he'll have a date.

We hear about Jim's thoughts only to the extent that we need to understand his motives.

We tend to think third person is a less intimate way to tell a story. But with a close perspective—as if the camera were sitting on the character's shoulder—third person can be as intimate as first. At the same time, a third person narrative can step back from any particular character to show the big picture.

Intimate, first-person narratives provide a powerful mode in which to tell stories of personal growth and development. But because the mode is self-centered, it's easy to cross the line into self-indulgence.

Third person excels at showing structures and patterns larger than any one individual. But greater scope usually means less engagement with the individuals in the story.

Regardless of trends or conventions—many young adult novels, for example, are written in first-person, something cynics say is appropriate because the subjects are self-obsessed—you should choose a narrative perspective that fits the model of your story. What it comes down to, as it usually does, is that you must use the right tool for the job, and not simply follow fashions.

THE SECOND RULE OF TWO: TWO CHOICES

Static models demonstrate relationships. Dynamic models show principles of operation. It's much easier to understand how something works if you see it in action than if you read a description.

You may think a book is a static model because its words don't change after it has been printed. But we experience the story through a linear narrative. Like movies, where the still pictures in individual frames move when viewed in rapid succession, books come alive as they unfold over time.

Stories become working models when they follow the second rule of two: a character doesn't show any character unless he or she has two real choices.

You might object that regardless of the situation the character can always choose to act differently. While true in principle, in practice many of those choices are not real choices: if the space aliens come, demanding that you obey or be exterminated, choosing to be exterminated is a choice that accomplishes little more than taking you out of the story.

We have a lot of stories in comics, TV, and movies, where the hero does the right thing because he or she is the hero. Simple stories like that do have an element of fun. But consider how much more it says if a character, which we've seen behave with both kindness and cruelty, chooses, at a critical moment, to be kind.

The key is to establish that the character has the capacity to go either way. Only when they're free to choose and capable of carrying out their choice do we see a working model of real character.

* * *

Give ten writers the same premise and you'll likely get ten different stories. That's because each writer will create a different model—emphasizing and omitting different things—out of the same initial elements. Even something that seems as simple as telling your story in first or third person can make a surprising difference.

Understanding stories as models gives you more artistic freedom because it provides a way for you to get out from under the inertia of your words. Other arts have more formal notions of play—sketches and studies, for example—but the effort required to string words together leaves us reluctant to discard any of that work. The story model you develop with a draft and refine through revisions gives you a framework for assessing whether a given element contributes to or detracts from the story. Constantly ask yourself what should be emphasized and what should be omitted to make the story clearer and more compelling.

CHAPTER 3.

MODELS VS. FORMULAS

There are two ways to learn how to make music: learn to read notation and master instrumental techniques so you can play the piece accurately, or fake it.

While it sounds like cheating, faking requires as much dedication and skill as traditional musicianship. Players who provide background music or take requests often rely on fake books—catalogs of popular pieces that show the lyrics, melody line, and chord changes for each song. Using their knowledge of music, particularly chording and rhythmic patterns, fakers improvise an appropriate accompaniment for the melody. When the lounge player answers a request with, "hum a few bars and I'll fake it," he or she isn't kidding.

Sheet music is a recipe for reproducing the song. The score lists every note in its temporal and harmonic association with all others. While there is room for interpretation and expression, the musician's job is essentially to reproduce, with voice or instrument, the music as specified.

Fake book notation provides a model of the song: it

emphasizes the essential elements that distinguish a song. No one would confuse the version of a song played by a faker with the original, but they'll recognize it as a reasonable facsimile.

As you look for guidance or advice on how to construct stories that are both satisfying and compelling, you need to understand the difference between recipes and models. The former help you reproduce something faithfully. The latter provide a pattern, but what you do with the pattern may look nothing like the original.

THE HOLLYWOOD FORMULA

One of the things you're likely to come across as you search for resources on story structure is the Hollywood formula. It's supposed to be the secret sauce with which successful movies are made.

If it works so well in visual media, why not use it for written storytelling?

At a high level, the formula breaks the ninety to one hundred and twenty minute runtime of a feature film into three acts:

- Act 1 = first quarter
- Act 2 = middle half
- Act 3 = last quarter

But what goes into each act?

You're in luck. There's no shortage of people willing to lay out the formula for you. Unfortunately, there is no single formula.

Here are two representative versions:

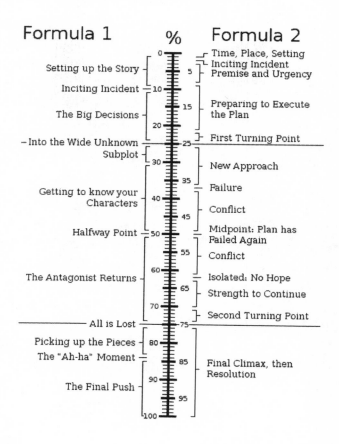

Setting aside obvious discrepancies in the timing of shared elements and divergent points of emphasis, both formulas feel rigid: if certain things don't happen by certain times, the formula—and, by extension, your story—falls apart.

It's also hard to set aside the suspicion that the formula will produce cookie-cutter stories.

Of course, the only question that really matters is

whether the formula provides the guidance you need in order to write your story. Do you know what the big decisions that follow the inciting incident in formula one should be? What about the two sections labeled, "conflict," that bracket the midpoint in formula two: do you know how the first differs from the second?

There are other versions of the Hollywood formula which break the elements outlined above into finer-grained steps. You can get as much detail as you wish. But no matter how well defined the elements, they're still slots into which you're supposed to plug your story. At best, the formula shows how to assemble a narrative.

What, then, should you do if you need guidance on the why of a story—the substance more than the form?

You might look to archetypes, like the Hero's Journey.

THE HERO'S JOURNEY

What does the Hero's Journey look like?

In the following figure, the hero moves counter-clockwise around the circle, starting at, "The Innocent World of Childhood," and completing the mythic cycle with, "Freedom to Live."

As interesting as it might be, a simple diagram isn't enough. Most of the steps require more explanation. Even ones that seem clear, like, "Dragon-battle," raise questions about how figurative or literal an episode in your story must be to count as a Hero's Journey—the answer, by the way, is, "yes," because with a mythic cycle, anything can work.

Here's a more straightforward version—to which we'll refer later:

1. The Ordinary World
2. The Call to Adventure
3. Refusing the Call
4. Meeting the Mentor
5. Crossing the Threshold
6. Tests, Allies, and Enemies
7. The Inmost Cave
8. The Ordeal
9. The Reward
10. The Road Back
11. The Resurrection
12. Return with the Elixir

And so it seems we've come to the opposite extreme from the cookie-cutter approach, where anything goes. Some people have tried to reduce the Hero's Journey to a recipe, arguing the correct cycle actually has 188 or 510 steps.

META MODELS

To be fair, I've presented the Hollywood Formula and the Hero's Journey as straw men in this chapter. There's more to both frameworks (in fact, I devote a substantial portion of another book on character and archetype to the hero and his journey). I've given you the outlines in a less than completely flattering light to illustrate the danger of confusing the model of a model (or meta model) with the model itself.

A story is a model in which you distill the complexities of real life (or a life that could be real in another world) into a coherent narrative. You can apply the same distillation process to many stories and come up with a model of what's common among those stories—in other words, a model of the original models. This is precisely how we got the Hollywood Formula (a model of movies) and the Hero's Journey (a model of myths).

The one thing you must understand is that a model is a pattern not a formula that guarantees a certain outcome if followed correctly. A pattern shows the relationships and relative proportions of the elements. Viewed in this light, the relative proportions of the acts in the Hollywood Formula reflect the fact that visual media excel at showing the protagonist working to solve the story problem (i.e., act two). Similarly, the Hero's Journey shows the pattern of stages through which the hero passes as he transforms from a callow and untested youth into someone capable of defeating the antagonist, but it doesn't mean that each step must have equal weight in a particular story.

* * *

Cooking is an interesting art. At one level, it's all about recipes—amassing thousands and thousands of them. And yet two cooks given the same recipe can produce dramatically different results. The success of a recipe depends on a host of external factors ranging from the quality and freshness of the ingredients to the altitude at which you cook. What distinguishes great cooks is that they know food and their kitchens so well they can make substitutions and improvise as necessary. For them, recipes are more like fake books than formulas.

We call long-form works of fiction novels because we're looking for something new—but not so radically different we don't know what to make of it. The key question is not how well you can follow a formula but rather what can you do to breathe life into a story model.

CHAPTER 4.

THREE IS A MAGIC NUMBER

I enjoy British sitcoms more than American ones.

There I said it.

And I'm prepared to face accusations of a lack of patriotism or, worse, elitism.

Part of it is the cultural distance: it's easier to believe people across the pond are like the ones I see in the programs because I don't rub shoulders with many counter-examples. Cultural distance is, however, even more important on a structural level. The British programming with which I'm most familiar has come to me through the good offices of various PBS stations, who presumably select the better material.

I also confess a weakness for the language. Between the accents and the slang, viewing British comedies is a more engaging experience because it requires some effort on my part to follow along. British sitcom writers seem to have a particular gift for articulate, literate, sarcasm.

But I think the most important reason for my preference is the format. Thanks to the commercial interruption, American sitcoms have two acts. Their British counterparts have only a single, longer act.

In addition to forcing the story into two acts, the American format requires the first act to end on a note strong enough to keep the viewer's interest during the commercial break. Then the second act must bring down the tension in order to have enough space to build to the climax of the story. In other words, American sitcoms must have two high points: a false climax at the end of the first act and the narrative climax at the end of the second.

In contrast, British sitcoms can spend the entire half-hour developing the characters and building the narrative tension toward a single, more natural climax.

This is why there's some truth to the generalization that British comedies are driven by character, while American comedies are driven by caricature. If you haven't watched any British sitcoms, you owe it to yourself as a writer to compare and contrast. It's an eye-opening exercise.

The point here, however, is not to argue for English superiority but to show how deeply structure affects storytelling.

CLASSIC STORY STRUCTURE

There are schemes laying out the structure of a story in such detail that it seems the writer's only job is to fill in the blanks. Whether it's the archetype of the hero's journey or the Hollywood formula, there are outlines with the fifteen to fifty elements that are supposed to be included in a paint-by-numbers story.

The **Star Trek Roleplaying Game Narrator's Guide**, for example, has a seven-point system [4]:

1. Hook
2. Plot Turn 1
3. Pinch 1
4. Midpoint
5. Pinch 2
6. Plot Turn 2
7. Resolution

This isn't too overwhelming, but what are pinches and midpoints and plot turns and so on?

Look at it this way:

- Action (cause) = Plot Turn or Midpoint
- Consequence (effect) = Pinch or Resolution

If we set aside the Hook as a special, initial case, we are left with three pairs of actions and consequences. The consequence in each of the first two pairs is called a Pinch because it doesn't resolve the story problem.

If we stand back and squint, after the hook introduces the story problem, we see:

- Plot Turn 1, the first attempt to solve the problem, causes Pinch 1, the effect of failing to resolve the story problem. Let's call this try/fail cycle, "Act one."
- The Midpoint is the second attempt to solve the problem and causes Pinch 2, which still doesn't resolve the story problem. Let's call this try/fail cycle, "Act two."

- Plot Turn 2 finally resolves the story problem and leads to the Resolution. We can call this try/succeed cycle, "Act Three."

"Wait!" you say. "This looks suspiciously like the dreaded Three-act Story Structure. What are you trying to pull?"

I am making a case for the three-act structure, not because it's the *One True Answer*, but because it is the clearest way to illustrate the basis of story theory: that story is the minimum container of significance.

But before we explore that idea, we need to address the elephant in the center ring—the thing writers who have trouble with the three-act structure fear the most: the middle.

REHABILITATING THE REPUTATION OF THE MIDDLE

In general, the problem most writers have with act two is that, with an intriguing beginning and a mind-blowing ending, the middle seems like little more than what you have to go through to get to the good stuff at the end.

The middle isn't simply the bridge between the beginning and the ending. It is what ties the two together. Specifically, the middle is where we see the protagonist grow and become the person able to rise to the challenges and overcome the antagonist in the end. The middle is where we most clearly see character development. If your protagonist at the beginning of the story is capable of defeating your antagonist, you have an incident, not a story.

Justine Musk explains the role of the middle this way:

"An important part and purpose of a story's middle act is revelation. The middle act, as Michael Halperin puts it, "is the central place where revelations, motivations, and confrontations take place—making the stories we create live and breathe." Information rises from that secret underside to raise the stakes, deepen character, and shift the reader's perceptions." [5]

Viewed in this light, the middle is arguably more important than the beginning or the end because it is the place in the story where the transformation occurs that makes the ending possible.

One of the reasons writers have trouble with middles is because they confuse complications and revelations. Complications, often in the form of a string of problems, are like trying to fly between busy airports where you spend more time—either on the runway waiting to take off or in a holding pattern waiting to land—than it takes to cover the distance to the destination. A revelation, to continue the travel analogy, is taking ground transport because you missed the flight, discovering you can get to the destination more quickly, and then using that fact later to help defeat the antagonist.

Look at your middles. Don't bloat them with empty complication calories. Test each scene in the middle and ask, "Does this scene reveal something the characters need to know or be by the end, or is it simply delaying the resolution?"

THREE IS A MAGIC NUMBER

If you take some time for a numeric inventory, you don't need **Schoolhouse Rock** to convince you that three is a magic number. [6] From the practical (it takes a minimum of three legs to create a free-standing structure like a tripod or a stool), through society (the framers of the constitution of the United States established three branches of government for the express purpose of creating check and balances), to the sacred (the Holy Trinity of Father, Son, and Holy Ghost), our world and our culture are rife with threes.

Three, however, goes deeper as a cultural template. We understand the old phrase, "lock, stock, and barrel," as a euphemism for completeness. These three parts define the whole because they refer to the three non-reducible components of a firearm (at least through the 19th century). But the list of three as an expression of wholeness goes much deeper into our cultural foundations. Popular songs usually have three parts: a first verse and chorus, a second verse and chorus, and then a bridge and a final chorus. Jokes often have three beats: a straight line, another straight line, and then the punch line—like volleyball, where the bump, set, and spike are the athletic equivalent of comedy. This is because you need at least three measurements to identify a trend.

Story is fundamentally about cause and effect. Most stories have at least three pairs of causes and effects. Why? Because a problem worthy of a story has to be hard enough that it takes more than one or two tries to find the solution.

THE GOLDILOCKS GUIDE TO ARTILLERY

The story of the three bears tells how their uninvited visitor sampled three kinds of ursine hospitality—porridge, chairs, and beds—and found in each a trinity of states: too hot, too cold, and just right.

Setting aside the deep and often disturbing psychological messages hidden in the simple stories we blithely repeat to our children, the little adventure with Goldilocks is a fair summary of the art of artillery prior to the advent of fire-control computers, range-finders, and the Global Positioning System. You see, the first shot often missed—perhaps falling short. So the artillerymen would adjust their settings and fire again—this time, perhaps, the shell might go long. With the target bracketed by shots that were too hot and too cold, the third shot was more likely to be just right.

While the process of zeroing in on a solution may, in fact, take more than three tries, the cliché about the third time being the charm is commonly true because that's how we tell stories.

Think about the do-it-yourself or home improvement project stories you've heard. As we discussed in the first chapter, these stories tend to have three beats:

1. You go to the store to get what you need
2. You go back to the store to get what you didn't know you need
3. You go once more to get what you really need

Why three beats? Because three is the minimum container for significance.

- One act or action is a rule: in this situation do the following.

- Two acts or actions demonstrate a procedure: try this, if that doesn't work, try that.

- Three acts or actions give us a story: not this, not that, but a third thing.

Like classic artillery, a story shows how the protagonist triangulated on the ultimate solution. In terms of cause and effect, of course, we want to know the solution, but it is the first two failed attempts that make the story significant. The first act demonstrates why the common rule or obvious response doesn't resolve the story problem. The second act shows why the fall-back procedures also don't work. These failures prove the story problem is non-trivial and that both the solution and the way in which the protagonist finds it are something the audience doesn't already know.

Three acts: three try/fail or cause-and-effect cycles, where, like beats of a classic joke, the first two set up the third. This is the whole of the mystery of story structure.

Don't assume, because the structural language above is abstract, that there's something lofty about three acts. The structure is a pattern, not a formula with which you must comply. It is nothing more than an explicit statement of something we know intuitively from a lifetime of hearing stories: good ones have a beginning, middle, and end.

- **Act One**: The beginning establishes the context, problem, and stakes.

- **Act Two**: The middle develops complications and revelations.

- **Act Three**: The end reveals the full scope of the problem and the final resolution.

CHAPTER 5.

COMPLEX STORIES ARE FRACTAL

Perfect order is completely regular and predictable. A screen showing a single color is perfectly orderly.

Complete chaos is perfectly random and predictably unpredictable. A screen showing noise is completely chaotic.

Perfect order and perfect chaos are also perfectly boring.

Stories where either nothing happens or everyone recognizes the problem and works together to solve it are also perfectly boring.

Narrative complexity is not an end, in and of itself. Your story should never be any more complex than it needs to be. But because of what you see and experience in the wider world, some degree of narrative complexity, particularly in long-form works like novels, is essential if you want your stories to ring true.

So how do you go about creating the right kind of complexity?

ORGANIC VS. ARTIFICIAL

The world around us, in all its intricate beauty, is a mix of order and chaos. Trees look like trees, yet no two are exactly alike. The word we use to describe the way in which related animals, plants, and even landscapes are similar but vary is, "organic." Something artificial, a word whose Latin roots mean, "contrived by art," sticks out from the natural background because it's too regular and too simple.

Rich ecosystems thrive in the dynamic equilibrium that arises on the boundary between order and chaos. The inter-tidal zone of the seashore is a good example: alternately a part of the chaos of the sea and the order of the land, the shore is home to a richer mix of life per unit area than you'll find on either side.

The secret, discovered and explained in mathematical terms only recently, is that organic complexity has structure and arises from surprisingly simple rules. For example, a computer can simulate the way in which a flock of birds or school of fish seems to move as one with only three simple rules:

1. Separation – avoid crowding neighbors (short range repulsion)
2. Alignment – steer toward the average heading of neighbors
3. Cohesion – steer toward the average position of neighbors (long range attraction) [7]

At each time step in the simulation, every bird uses these rules to determine how to adjust its course and speed. The complex aggregate behavior of the flock arises from repeatedly applying these simple rules.

Many kinds of complexity, both natural and artificial, are the product of simple rules applied repeatedly. Stories are no exception. In a simple sense, the rounds of editing and revision involve the repeated application of the relatively simple rules of grammar and clear expression. But the principle has more profound implications at the structural level.

STRUCTURE

As a child, the eminent nineteenth-century mathematician Carl Friedrich Gauss was assigned, along with the rest of his class, to add the numbers from one to one hundred—perhaps because his teacher wanted some quiet time. While the other students scribbled furiously on their slates, Gauss cocked his head, stared into space for a minute, wrote a number on his slate, and delivered the correct answer to the teacher (who, I suspect, wasn't thrilled by the prodigy).

Unlike his industrious class mates, who set to adding the numbers sequentially, Gauss noticed an underlying pattern: if you fold the number line back on itself, pivoting at fifty, each pair of numbers (0 and 100, 1 and 99, ... 49 and 51) adds up to one hundred. There are fifty pairs of numbers. That and the fifty at the pivot point gave Guass the answer: 5050.

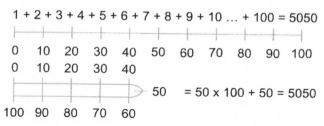

Add all the numbers from 1 to 100.

$1 + 2 + 3 + 4 + 5 + 6 + 7 + 8 + 9 + 10 \ldots + 100 = 5050$

0	10	20	30	40	50	60	70	80	90	100

0	10	20	30	40

50     $= 50 \times 100 + 50 = 5050$

100	90	80	70	60

Structure is nothing more or less complicated than the relationships implicit in something. Those relationships create distinctions that may not be obvious. For example, shark skin feels smooth if you pet from nose to tail but acts like sand paper if you go the other way. This is because the skin, which looks uniform from a distance, is made up of overlapping, tooth-like plates that point toward the tail.

We often say something is complex when we don't understand what's happening or how it works. A piece of music where different instruments seem to be going off in any number of directions may seem complex to a listener trying to take it all in for the first time, but if you study the score you discover the structure, from the fundamental timing and rhythm to mid-level organizing principles like eight-bar sections, to the melodic figures and motifs that recur. Even things like Celtic illuminations or exquisite arabesques are composed of simpler patterns made more complex through repetition and variation.

The narrative complexity you want is the kind that delights readers by filling their literary senses with the world of your story, not the kind that frustrates and confuses because it is impenetrable. In fact, what you readers find to be intriguingly complex should seem simple to you because, like Gauss, you understand the patterns.

DYNAMICS

The other essential aspect of the organic world is that it is dynamic: it changes over time. It's no accident that music is an excellent way to illustrate both structure and dynamics because, like the world around us, we experience it in time.

The conceptual break-through that created the mathematics of fractals (which makes possible the photo-realistic computer graphics that permeate our visual media) was the addition of time. Iterative systems use the result of one step to calculate the next. By applying the same steps over and over, we can create remarkably intricate patterns.

The following figure shows steps two through five in the generation of a Koch snowflake:

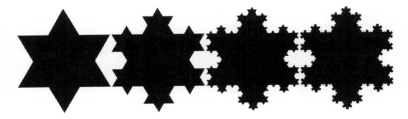

Beginning with a triangle, the generator takes each line segment in the perimeter, divides it into three sub-segments, and replaces the middle segment with two others of the same length to form a triangle in the middle of the line. With only five iterations, we have the outline of something you might enjoy catching on your tongue.

FRACTAL SELF-SIMILARITY

In simple terms, self-similarity means that the parts look like the whole. A twig, for example, looks like a branch, and a branch looks like a tree. The computer-generated fern frond below was created by adding copies of the overall shape that have been scaled, stretched, rotated, and mirrored.

But a hallmark of natural systems is that the copies are not exact: overall, the forms are similar, showing a degree of order, and yet chaos introduces variations in details like the branch point and angle.

Stories must have a beginning, middle, and end. If we look again at the most common twelve-step formulation of the Hero's Journey, it's not difficult to see how each set of four steps maps into acts that at a broad brush level cover the beginning, middle, and end of the hero's transformative journey.

The Hero's Journey

	1. The Ordinary World
Act I	2. The Call to Adventure
	3. Refusing the Call
	4. Meeting the Mentor
	5. Crossing the Threshold
Act II	6. Tests, Allies, & Enemies
	7. The Inmost Cave
	8. The Ordeal
	9. The Reward
Act III	10. The Road Back
	11. The Resurrection
	12. Return with the Elixir

But look more closely: within each act we see a beginning, middle, and end.

The Hero's Journey

Act I	Beginning	1. The Ordinary World
		2. The Call to Adventure
	Middle	3. Refusing the Call
	End	4. Meeting the Mentor

Act II	Beginning	5. Crossing the Threshold
		6. Tests, Allies, & Enemies
	Middle	7. The Inmost Cave
	End	8. The Ordeal

Act III	Beginning	9. The Reward
		10. The Road Back
	Middle	11. The Resurrection
	End	12. Return with the Elixir

In a short story, you only have time for one beginning, middle, and end. Long-form narratives can develop fractal self-similarity because they have beginnings, middles, and ends at many levels:

- Novels have a beginning, middle, and end, usually made up of acts.
- Acts have a beginning, middle, and end, usually made up of groups of chapters.

- Groups of chapters have a beginning, middle, and end, usually made up of chapters.

- Chapters have a beginning, middle, and end, usually made up of scenes.

- Scenes have a beginning, middle, and end.

- Paragraphs have a beginning, middle, and end.

- Sentences have a beginning, middle, and end.

That's seven levels of nested beginnings, middles, and ends. It may seem overwhelming until you step back and see that it's simply a matter of understanding that each beginning, middle, and end has its own beginning, middle, and end.

You don't have to keep all of that in mind as you write. If you simply remember that the particular beginning, middle, and end on which you're working is a part of the beginning, middle, or end of something larger, the narrative complexity that makes a long-form story rich and lush will flow naturally.

This, by the way is why people agonize over chapter one, scene one: it's the beginning (scene) of the beginning (chapter) of the beginning (chapter group) of the beginning (act) of the beginning (novel). That scene must start the story at a number of fractal levels—so, no pressure, right?

Think about it this way: in an ideal world, a perfect protagonist moves directly from the story problem to the solution. In the real world, as we discussed in the last chapter, we try to solve the problem and fail at least twice before we hit upon the real solution. If we graph the too-hot/too-cold/just-right pattern of acts over time, it might look like this:

Of course, no one proceeds directly from the beginning of an act to its conclusion. Each act is made up of smaller steps that are attempts to solve the problems and reach the objectives at that level. For example, in the beginning of **The Lord of the Rings**, the hobbits are only concerned with getting themselves and the ring to Rivendell. With no clue as to the larger problems awaiting them once they arrive, Frodo and his friends stumble from one peril to another as they attempt the journey.

But each of those episodes has its own beginning, middle, and end as the hobbits try to understand and work their way out of each new predicament.

With only three levels of beginning, middle, and end, our smooth trajectory from problem to solution has turned into a complex trajectory.

TIME AND SPACE

The final ingredient in narrative complexity is dispersion in time and space. In the world around us, things don't all begin at the same time or in the same space. While much of the natural world is necessarily synchronized with celestial rhythms like day and night and the turn of the seasons, the vibrant complexity we see and feel is the collective result of countless beginnings, middles, and ends going on everywhere right now. The early flowers, for example, wilt to make way for the late bloomers.

In your stories this means plot elements and character arcs should start and end at different times and places. Again, in **The Lord of the Rings**, the final act of Gandalf's arc begins when he determines Frodo has the One Ring, while the first act of Frodo's story doesn't really get underway for several more months. As the hobbits, and the readers, become aware of some of the things that have happened and are happening they realize the world is larger and more complex than they ever imagined.

COMPLEX NARRATIVES IN THREE SIMPLE STEPS

Given how liberally I've used examples from J.R.R.

Tolkien's opus, you may despair of ever doing anything comparable because you'll never have twenty years to invent myths and languages enough to fill a fictional world. But the real secret to producing complex narratives has been sitting there right in front of your face on the shampoo bottle each time you shower:

1. **Lather**: break plot and character arcs into beginnings, middles, and ends.
2. **Rinse**: distribute the beginnings, middles, and ends of the plot and character arcs in story space and time.
3. **Repeat**: do it all over at successively smaller scales.

* * *

Of course, no one is going to complain about lack of fractal character when they critique your manuscript. And consciously trying to make your story fractal will feel terribly artificial. As with other aspects of the art of writing, it's something to internalize. But if you develop an eye for the patterns and parallels that create similarity at different narrative levels your stories will naturally become richer and more satisfying.

CHAPTER 6.

STORY DRIVERS

If story were best understood in terms of aeronautical engineering, this chapter would be about thrust and the next, on conflict, would be about drag.

Without conflict, there is no story—all you have is an *I-wanted-something-so-I-got-it* statement. But without the, "I wanted," or, "I needed," you also have no story. If nothing is amiss, nothing needs to change. There must be some need or drive that motivates the protagonist to act. Even stories that start with, "I was minding my own business when …" are driven by the implicit need to survive or restore the situation to normal.

Stories are funny things because they take place in the minds of the people hearing or reading them. This means stories unfold at both the explicit level of the characters in the narrative and at the implicit level of the reader as they experience the story. The first level is driven by the logic of the story—do the characters seem real and well-motivated? The second level is driven by reader engagement—does the reader care, or worry, enough about the characters and their situation to keep reading?

STORY LOGIC: MIND THE GAP

The London Underground is filled with signs encouraging passengers to, "Mind the Gap," between the platform and the car. This subway signage is also good advice for writers looking for internal story drivers.

Story arises from the gap between expectations and outcomes. The protagonist does something but the result is not what he or she expected—the story problem not only remains unresolved, it has become worse—so they're forced to try something else. Those gaps propel characters forward into the next try/fail cycle and the story continues until, in the crucible of the final conflict, the protagonist bridges the most important gaps.

Gaps of all sorts can lead to stories. At the level of setting, for example, places where different biomes, topographies, or cultures meet— like an oasis surrounded by different groups of people who want or need to control the water—create gaps at the point of transition. In terms of character, the gap between a person's desire to protect a loved one and their inability to do so might drive them to wreak bloody vengeance.

Put another way, if everything is continuous and predictable, characters know what to do and there's no story. It's only when there's a gap in continuity—a cause with an unanticipated effect—that we have a story worth telling.

A THEORY OF STORY DRIVERS

Gaps are necessary but not sufficient. We all notice when something turns out differently than we expected, but without a strong motive to solve the problem we often give up. The most interesting characters bring an uncommon passion to the story and its problem. It's the protagonist's story because he or she is the only one who has the drive to bridge the gap between problem and solution.

Passion is a mixed blessing: too little and we have a lifeless story, too much and readers recoil from the irrationality. Passion in characters must be tempered by clarity, necessity, and purpose. The protagonist's plight—what is at stake and why it matters—must be vivid in the minds of both characters and readers. Readers need to believe the struggle is necessary and that the actions of the characters driving the story forward are purposeful. If either of these ingredients is missing, readers will doubt the story or the storyteller.

Every element in the narrative— setting, character, and plot—should drive the story forward. Elements are compelling to the degree that they are vivid, necessary, and purposeful.

The following questions illustrate how to assess your story drivers:

Setting
Vivid: Can you see it? Do you want to be there?

Necessary: Is it clear that the story couldn't happen anywhere else?

Purposeful: Does the setting feel natural and not contrived?

Character
Vivid: Are the characters distinct, interesting, and memorable?

Necessary: Does each character have a reason for being part of the story (i.e., no red-shirts or Mary-Sues [8])?

Purposeful: Does each character go somewhere (i.e. grow or change) in the story? Are they affected by the events?

Plot

Vivid: Is it clear what's going on? And why?

Necessary: Do the plot points make sense? Do they matter? (i.e., it's not a plot point if the character could clear up a misunderstanding with a five minute conversation.)

Purposeful: Does the plot go somewhere that rewards the reader for the time they've invested? Does it end in a place that feels both surprising and inevitable?

COMPELLING AND ENTICING

Story drivers affect readers in one of two ways.

Consider the structural difference between a thriller and a mystery:

A thriller is compelling; it pushes you along. From the beginning, we need to know what's at stake because a thriller is a story about an effort to avert some peril. Worry about how to prevent the worst outcome drives this kind of story forward.

A mystery, in contrast, **is enticing; it pulls you along**. It is a story of discovery in which the scope of the peril is revealed over time. Worry about what might be hiding just out of sight drives this kind of story forward.

Thrillers are usually set in the real world because the author can use common knowledge and convention to establish the stakes. In a political thriller, for example, it is sufficient to say the conspirators are working to topple the government and proceed on the assumption that readers agree such an outcome would be a bad thing.

At the other end of the spectrum, fantastic stories are rarely thrillers—unless one relies on familiar genre conventions (which is why urban fantasies and paranormal romances do well)—because readers can't appreciate what's at stake until they understand the new world. In fact, because of the degree of novelty, most fantasies are not just mysteries in an abstract sense but explicitly involve some form of discovery, like a quest or voyage.

You must be clear about the kind of story you're telling because if you mix them up you'll deliver a thrill-less thriller or a mystery with no mystery.

Of course, few stories rely entirely on either enticement or compulsion. Most employ a mix. In **The Empire Strikes Back**, for example, first we worry because we don't know what's going to happen to Han Solo when he's frozen in carbonite, and then, a few minutes later when Darth Vader lures Luke into the freezing chamber, we worry because we know exactly what's going to happen. Done right, you can make your readers worry about what they know as well as what they don't know.

Buy why do you want your readers to worry?

Because that's how you draw them into the story.

SEDUCING READERS

Well-crafted stories are actually a hierarchy of enticements and compulsions: the first line encourages the reader to read the first paragraph; the first paragraph launches them through the first page; the first page pulls them into the first chapter; and so on.

As a principle, this seems like a sound and effective approach. But how do you pull it off in practice? How do you seduce readers into the heart of the story?

Consider what Stephenie Meyer did with **Twilight**. At a structural level, she used a small mystery to lure the reader into a larger mystery. Specifically, every-girl Bella arrives in Forks expecting to have a hard time fitting in. Contrary to her assumptions, everybody likes her—except one aloof boy who seems to hate her for no apparent reason and yet saves her life. This setup creates an irresistible emotional mystery for the book's target audience: what could possibly explain the anomalous behavior? The answer to that question opens the door to the larger problems of the vampire story.

Love or loath **Twilight**, you have to admit it produced a strong reaction among its readers—like an emotional drug. Seduction, like addiction, proceeds in increments, with each step drawing you further in. While perhaps not the most morally upstanding analogy, seduction is an excellent model to follow as you structure your stories.

BALANCING ACTION AND INFORMATION

Seduction depends on the seducer being subtle and patient. In the movie **Willow**, when the warrior Madmortigan tries to evade the authorities by dressing as a woman and hiding in a tavern, a drunken mountain of a man corners him and, demonstrating the antithesis of seduction, makes an irresistible proposition, "I'm Lunk. Wanna breed?" [9]

The most skillful seducers make their subjects believe it was their idea all along. The most skillful storytellers make their readers believe they are participating in the story as it unfolds—that it's the first time for both of them.

A critical part of the way in which the author seduces readers is through the balance of action and information in the story. If you start with action—explosions! riots! mortal combat!—your readers won't have any reason to root for the hero (aside from the fact that he or she is the hero) and will likely be confused. If you start with an exposition about each character, his or her backstory, and their situation at the beginning of the book, readers will likely lose interest before anything happens.

The best practice is to weave action and information together: start with a small action that, in addition to its intrinsic interest, provides a way to share some information with the reader. Of course, both action and information are most interesting if they also tell us something about the characters.

It may seem you have less information to convey to readers if your story doesn't take place in a fantastic setting. And yet, upon closer examination, the amount of information readers need in order to appreciate a story set in the real world is essentially the same: in order to care, readers need to know what's at stake, but in order to know what's at stake readers need to understand the nature of the world. With fantasy, you clearly have the burden of introducing readers to a world that contradicts or extends their common experience. With a realistic story, you have an analogous burden of introducing readers to the particular world of the characters: your protagonist may have a dangerous and exotic job, but why, out of all the people who have that job, should we care about this particular person?

* * *

The difference between an unremarkable book and one you can't put down is worry—the degree to which readers are reluctant to stop when they're reading, and continue to think about the story when they aren't.

We call it, "getting pulled into a book," for a good reason. Readers who have been pulled into a book put their need to follow the story ahead of other needs, like sleep. They do so because they accept the necessity of the story. Fascinating characters confronted with compelling and enticing story problems—and whose motives for solving those problems feel necessary to readers—drive the story unfolding in readers minds. Tap into those deep veins of necessity and your readers won't be able to put down your book.

CHAPTER 7.

CONFLICT

It's thrilling to watch the star-fighters swoop and roll through space battles in **Star Wars**. That's why it's a let-down when physicists point out such things would never happen in the vacuum of space. The graceful but deadly ballet of aerial combat that inspired George Lucas is only possible because of atmospheric drag.

If motivation and necessity are the drivers that thrust a story forward, conflict is the drag that gives the story an interesting arc and enables it to go somewhere worthwhile.

ORGANIC CONFLICT

In comic books, bad guys are bad simply because they're bad. Slap on a label like, "Nazi," or, "Terrorist," and your job is done, right? Other examples of stereotypical antagonists include oppressive clergy, greedy corporations, and government conspiracies. They're bad, so the protagonists fighting against them must be good. It's conflict by definition, which is always a contrivance.

Another kind of contrived conflict is irrational conflict:

characters at loggerheads whose differences could be resolved with a brief conversation. Romances are particularly liable to this kind of contrivance when the author can't think of a better reason to keep the couple apart. Yes, misunderstandings occur in real life, as do coincidences, but as a general rule you're only allowed one of each in a novel.

Of course, it's not that some kinds of conflict are contrived and others are not. Any conflict where the reader sees the puppet strings, or worse, the puppeteer, is contrived. Readers need to believe that the conflict in the story is necessary—that it arises organically from the mix of setting, plot, and characters—and inevitable—that it couldn't have played out any other way. Organic conflict, whether it's driven by characters or plot, is like a force of nature: picture the surge of the restless sea meeting an immovable cliff, or a speeding car meeting a brick wall.

NARRATIVE CONFLICT AND NECESSITY

One of the truisms of storytelling is that your protagonist is only as good as your antagonist. If, like the Monty Python self-defense class sketch, your antagonist threatens everyone with ... wait for it ... a banana(!), and your protagonist uses his pistol to save the day, we've learned nothing from the story—except that you should carry a gun if you're likely to be attacked by fruit-wielding maniacs—because the only stretching the protagonist was forced to do involved reaching for his holster. [10]

Part of what makes stories superior to daily life is the presence of a clearly defined villain. You may object that there are plenty of stories where the villain doesn't have a face or is something that can't be embodied in a single person. But even those stories reveal the nature of the antagonistic forces and show how the protagonist overcomes them.

Conflict is the drag that forces the story engine to rev. That's why a great deal of writing advice boils down to, "Ratchet up the conflict." But you can't have engaging narrative conflict if the parties and their conflicting objectives are not clear.

When story should motivate as well as entertain, the need for a clear-cut antagonist is even more pressing. If you were told two stories, one about puppies who learn they should be nice to each other, and one about oppression and wrongs to be righted in your very own neighborhood, which is more likely to move you to do something?

The crux of the motivational problem is that we live in a world whose name, if we had to follow the branding precedent of a large, U.S.-based toy retailer, could be, "Ambiguities-R-Us." Uncertainty is paralyzing. You need a clearly-defined enemy to move your audience to action. During the Cold War, one of the partisan battle fields in the U.S. political arena was the tug-of-war (pun intended) over who was strongest on defense (i.e., who would stand up to the Soviet Union). Since the collapse of the Soviet Union, we've had a parade of mostly Middle Eastern dictators and terrorists, who have provided only a nebulous threat. Without a strong and consistent external threat, we have no choice but to look inward and create even more fearful threats at home—all of which are embodied by the other political party.

While it would be nice if our political narratives were more rational and enlightened—or simply more tolerant—they illustrate something we, as storytellers, should understand:

- Unambiguous conflict motivates action;
- The greater the conflict the more extraordinary the action.

CONFLICT AND THE MORAL HIGH GROUND

The U.S. Marines believe warfare is fundamentally a clash of wills, and that the party with the stronger one ultimately prevails. A significant part of the will to fight and win depends upon seizing the moral high ground.

The party forced to fight usually begins the conflict on the moral high ground, whereas the party that starts the fight has an uphill battle in the moral landscape to show why their aggression is justified. This is why so many stories start when the antagonist does something that threatens the protagonist's world. The protagonist starts with the moral high ground because they are forced to respond to the antagonist's actions.

This pattern is clearest in stories of overt conflict, but it applies equally in stories about characters where the conflicts are primarily emotional. The character that is forced to resolve a difficult situation is more sympathetic than the character that chooses to cause the situation.

Keep this in mind as you develop your protagonist and your antagonist. The one who is forced into a conflict will usually be more sympathetic than the one who chooses to cause the conflict.

INNER, PERSONAL, AND UNIVERSAL CONFLICT

When discussing narrative conflict, we often say there are only three kinds: inner, personal, and universal.

Let's look at the kinds of stories you get with the nine combinations of the inner, personal, and universal conflict. In the following table, read from the protagonist's row to the antagonist's column. For example, if the protagonist's concerns are primarily internal and the antagonists are personal, you have a coming-of-age story or a story about establishing one's place and identity.

	Antagonist Inner	Antagonist Personal	Antagonist Universal
Protagonist INNER	Psycological Drama	Coming-of-age, Establishing one's Place and Identity	Sociopath or Super Man
Protagonist Personal	Intervention and Healing	Romance, Mystery, Thriller, Speculative Fiction, etc. (i.e., most kinds of Narrative Conflict)	Rebels and Underdogs
Protagonist Universal	Fatalists and Extremists	Order vs. Chaos (Anti-rebellion)	Epic and Political Struggles

What I find interesting about this exercise is that the primary locus of conflict in most stories falls in the center square (personal vs. personal). Many other stories fall on the diagonal (inner vs. inner or universal vs. universal). Asymmetric stories (e.g., personal vs. universal), are rarer.

As social animals, personal conflicts are the easiest to understand. Even if your story involves inner or universal conflict, your narrative will generally be most effective if you can put a face on the enemy for your readers. Your band of freedom fighters may be up against an entire empire, but your readers will respond more strongly to the dark lord who makes finding them his personal quest than to the legions of faceless soldiers he deploys. Similarly, readers will find a psychological struggle more accessible if there are other actors who symbolize the inner conflict.

It's also interesting to consider where different genres cluster in the matrix. For example, romance and mystery generally land in the upper left quadrant while speculative fiction and thrillers land in the lower right. All of them, of course, overlap in the middle.

Stories, clearly, aren't limited to one kind of conflict, so this analysis is only useful when we're considering the primary conflict. Still, the moral of this little story is that conflict is best when it's personal.

NEED, IMPEDIMENT, ACTION, AND RESOLUTION

With all this talk of conflict, you may think your job is simply to pile on the unpleasantness—make the waiters rude, the ex-spouse spiteful, the superiors petty and vindictive, sprinkle in some bar fights, and generally make life a living hell for your protagonist.

More, however, is not better: it's the quality, not the quantity, of the conflict that shapes the story. As with any other narrative element, conflict that doesn't move the story forward has no more place in your book than a description of your character waking up and going about their morning preparations before leaving for work.

Meaningful conflict has four components: a need, an impediment, more than one possible course of action, and a resolution. Without all four elements, the conflict will ultimately prove meaningless.

NEED

As much as we may like the image of the tough guy or gal who takes no crap and never backs down, the best way to handle conflict is to avoid it altogether. Lawyers, for example, prefer to plea-bargain because trials, particularly ones with juries, are unpredictable. Even if you're likely to win the fight because you're bigger and stronger, you still risk getting injured in the process if you come to blows.

This is why antagonists who are bad by definition ring hollow. With the possible exception of sociopaths, no one chooses direct conflict if there's another way to get what they want because conflict of any sort takes effort.

The need to stay in the fight begins with the necessity that drives the story, but is focused and sustained by constraint or justification. Survival is a compelling need, particularly when the opposing forces are faceless. However, a sense of the rightness of your cause—especially if it is a selfless one, like a parent protecting a child—is an even more powerful compulsion.

IMPEDIMENT

Something must stand in the way of what the main

character needs. If there is no impediment, there is no conflict and likely no story.

The impediment is the obvious element of conflict. The antagonist almost always provides the impediment, but it could also be something external like a force of nature.

One of the villainous clichés is that at some point, usually right before he or she is about to dispatch the hero, the antagonist acknowledges the protagonist as a, "worthy adversary." While it may seem as hackneyed as the super villain's monologue that gives the super hero time to escape from the slow-acting, escape-proof death trap, establishing the protagonist and antagonist as worthy opponents is structurally necessary: conflicts where the parties are thoroughly mismatched are rarely interesting.

You don't need much of a hero if Larry the Messenger of Doom surrenders when he gets a paper-cut. Conversely, you don't have a hero if the antagonist disintegrates him or her the first time they meet. Of course, we do like our heroes to be the underdog because that gives them the moral high-ground. And many stories start with the apparent mismatch of a lone champion standing against all the forces of evil. That disparity, however, is what affords the hero scope to prove they are, in fact, worthy opponents.

MULTIPLE COURSES OF ACTION

"I have an antagonist, so I have conflict, so I have a story, right?"

It's not that simple. If your protagonist has no other options, then you still don't have a story. Remember, as a primitive how-to, a story tells us what to do in a similar situation. If there's only one course of action, then you have a fact, like, "If you step off a cliff, you will fall," not a story.

It's also not a story if the situation is resolved by events beyond your control. A story like, "I was poor, and then I won the lottery," doesn't tell anyone else how to reliably change his or her state from poor to rich.

Meaningful conflict is an important application of the second rule of two. Character is revealed through choices. The way in which the characters choose to carry out the conflict tells us more about them than whether they win or lose. Even in a fight to the death, characters can choose how to fight.

There may not be much choice in a particular confrontation—a character who is trapped may have only one way out—but through the arc of the conflict and its try/fail cycles, the protagonist should explore different courses of action.

RESOLUTION

A story is more than simply a relation of cause and effect, but if the narrative doesn't show how some course of action removed the impediment and satisfied the need then it's still not a story. This is what we mean when we say a story, "goes somewhere," or, conversely, complain that it doesn't go anywhere.

The need for narrative resolution is clearer when we focus on conflict. As a child, I had a ring-side seat for a war between the Central American nations of Honduras and El Salvador. A soccer match was the apparent catalyst that turned an acrimonious border dispute into an invasion. And then, after four days, the combatants ran out of men, materials, and money and the war sputtered to a stop. Nothing was resolved, aside from proving that neither side could afford to settle the matter on the battlefield. [11]

The real world is obviously full of pointless conflict. There are times and places where people kill each other because they know no other way. But readers turn to fiction for the clarity and resolution of a story model: why purchase or read your book if it gives them nothing more than what they get for free on the nightly news?

There is a special case, the cautionary tale, in which you want to show why nothing works and admonish your listeners to avoid the situation entirely. But in general, only stories with solutions have value for their listeners.

This is not to say that everything needs to be wrapped up and tied with a bow. Living with ambiguity is an important part of maturity. What we mean when we say we want resolution is that we need to understand the significance of the conflict and why the pain and effort were ultimately meaningful. Readers don't expect you to give them the answers to life, the universe, and everything, but they do expect that your story and the conflict driving it won't waste their time.

CHAPTER 8.

THE ART OF THE LONG FORM

Many people think they should write a book. If you can run a hundred yards, no one assumes you should also be able to run a marathon. But with writing, perhaps because we use words all the time, we tend to assume it's simply a matter of scaling up the number of words to produce a book.

The fact that you can string words into sentences, sentences into paragraphs, and paragraphs into a coherent narrative doesn't necessarily mean that you can or should keep doing it for 300 – 400 pages. Even if you can pen lyrical descriptions, whip out sparkling dialog, and present a good scene, it doesn't follow that you can sustain a novel-length story.

The first question to consider when you begin to explore the long form is whether you have enough of a story to sustain the narrative. Is your story problem sufficiently interesting and challenging? If your protagonist is hungry and then makes a sandwich, you don't have a novel—you don't even have a story. On the other hand, if your protagonist is hungry and has just crashed in the middle of the desert, you could fill a novel with the story of how he or she survives.

According to Donald Maass, a fully developed premise includes:

1. "A setting, milieu or world that is intriguingly different or unique;
2. "A central conflict that's bigger than the main character, or universal;
3. "A conflict that's personified (turned into people);
4. "A powerful inciting action;
5. "Choices for the above and all the story elements to follow that eschew the obvious, go for what's less obvious, take a counter-intuitive approach or simply are the opposite of one's first choice." [12]

Maass's final point, that your story and all its elements must eschew the obvious, is a bellwether of how well you will fulfill your obligation to get and keep readers' attention through the entire course of your book. It's not simply that if you choose obvious story elements you run the risk readers have been-there-and-done-that and may set your book aside in favor of something fresh, it's that you will have to work much harder to make those elements interesting and develop them into story problems readers can't dismiss. People become accustomed to constant stimulus. You must be able to increase the stimulus of the story problem over time in order to maintain readers' interest.

Clint Johnson said:

"Generally, when we talk about writing, we look at the components of story piecemeal. But knowing the pieces doesn't mean that you know how to put them together to function as a whole."

Having a story worthy of a book only means you're ready to begin exploring the long form. You may think a novel is easy because its chapters are like a string of short stories. There are, of course, some novels which fit that description, but what distinguishes long-form work, whether feature films, symphonies, or novels (to name a few), from the short form is that the whole is greater than the sum of the parts.

A work in the long form can be more meaningful than shorter forms if the author uses the time and space afforded by the form to create more contexts. Consider a symphony where a motif reappears juxtaposed with a different theme and the music takes on new meaning, or the way two people who have known each other a long time can speak volumes with a word, a gesture, or even a glance.

TRAJECTORY

Ever since Albert Einstein became the modern icon of brainiacs, we assume Isaac Newton has been superseded and can be safely put out to pasture with other outdated scientific figureheads. Because it seems so obvious, and because so much of the modern world is founded upon it, we forget that Newton's theory of universal gravity was as mind-blowing in its day as relativity is in ours. Among the many things for which we have Newton to thank, ballistics—or the science of dropping ordnance on your enemies—ranks near the top.

Ballistics is all about trajectory. Using Newton's laws of motion, we can predict the path a projectile launched with a certain force in a given direction will follow and thus determine where it will land.

Trajectory is also the heart of the art of the long form. Your reader is like a projectile and the story is the arc that will bring them to a certain emotional and conceptual target.

As long as your reader believes it's taking them somewhere interesting, they'll stay with the story. As an author, therefore, you must know the end from the beginning. And like Michelangelo who revealed the statue hidden in the block of marble by removing the waste, you must clear away anything that that could pull your readers out of the trajectory of the novel.

This means that you must, at some level, understand the trajectory. It doesn't matter whether you come to that understanding before you draft because you are an architect and have outlined everything, or after many drafts because you are a gardener. Unless you're Samuel Beckett, a long form work must go somewhere. From the moment the inciting incident launches your reader into the story, they must be on a trajectory that will bring them to the narrative climax just as surely as a shell fired from a canon will hit the target.

TENSION AND RELEASE

I have an album of selections from a classical oratorio, each of which is reinterpreted by powerful contemporary singers and musicians. Individually, the songs are amazing, but I can't listen to more than a few at a time:

each performance is so energetic they quickly wear me out.

A basic tenet of storytelling is that things must always get worse. This is what we mean by phrases like, "build toward the climax." How you do so is one of the fundamental arts of the long form.

The original DuPont powder mills, in Delaware, were situated along the Brandywine Creek, which powered the water wheels. Moving the heavy wagons loaded with raw materials and milled black powder between the uplands and the river bed seemed impossible because no team could pull the load all the way up the slope. The engineers solved this problem by building a wagon road made up of small slopes interspersed with level stretches, like a stairway. The horses were able to haul the loads up the succession of inclines if they rested a bit on the level sections.

Many popular songs use a verse-chorus-verse-chorus-bridge-chorus format. The choruses usually have more energy than the verses, giving listeners an experience that alternates between lower and higher tension. Then the bridge comes, releasing the tension of the preceding chorus but building a new kind of tension before exploding into the climax of the final chorus.

I'll bet you've never considered the similarities between music and wagon roads. That's okay because it's now time to add fish to the mix.

The techniques of tension and release in the long-form story are much like the patient fisherman playing out line and then reeling in his catch, bringing the fish a bit closer to the boat each time. Similarly, each relaxation cycle should release some but not all of the tension so that the next tense episode builds on the unreleased tension to take readers to a new high. Together, tension and release move the reader through the story, keeping their interest with variety and treading a skillful line between wearing them out with too much tension and boring them with too little.

This pattern of tension and release may sound as though it runs counter to our discussion of trajectory. But that's only because we've changed our metaphorical zoom level. A graph of average tension over story time should show steady growth to the climax until the denouement brings the final release.

Skillfully done, the cycles of tension and release are the visceral foundation of the experience your readers want from long-form stories. They'll experience many things vicariously through your characters, but they'll experience the tension and release directly.

VARIATION

Have you ever been with a child who wanted to watch the same movie or sing the same song over and over?

Did you survive the ordeal without needing medication or counseling?

Doing the same thing over and over quickly becomes tedious. This is why picture books are so hard to do well. Only the most masterful are still tolerable on their fiftieth reading.

But variation is more than simply changing things. Wikipedia says:

> "In music, variation is a formal technique where material is repeated in an altered form. The changes may involve harmony, melody, counterpoint, rhythm, timbre, orchestration or any combination of these." [13]

Of course, the listener must be able to recognize both the theme and the ways in which it has changed in order to appreciate the variation.

The three-act structure, with try-fail cycles embedded in each act, is, in a sense, simply three variations on the theme of solving the story problem. The arc of interactions between two characters is a series of variations on the theme of their relationship. Multiple characters trying to achieve the same goal embody strategic variations.

Some long-form literary writing is a self-conscious exercise in variations of a symbol or image. There are commercial writers, at the opposite end of the spectrum, who would swear on a stack of dime-store novels that they never allow nonsense like that to interfere with a good story. Wherever you fall on that spectrum, there's a natural way to use variation to enrich your long-form narrative: simply identify a basic element in your story and look for places where variations of that element might surface.

For example, if romantic love is an important part of your story, you could compare and contrast kinds of attachments from lust to devotion. Or, turning to the dark side, your story of revenge could include everything from lashing out in the heat of the moment to the Klingon-inspired, dish best served cold.

Abstractions work as well as emotions. Light can run from blinding to illuminating; truth, from absolute to relative; and knowledge from certainty to uncertainty.

As with music, variations only work when the reader can recognize the relationship between variations and thus appreciate the similarities and differences.

As a practical matter, don't get hung up on variations as an abstract exercise or as a way to show future English-lit students how clever you are. The point of the story is the story. Use variations to make the story richer and more compelling, but never as an end in and of themselves.

RHYTHM

In a study of learning in babies and toddlers, investigators observed their subjects acting like little scientists, discovering their world by comparing hypothesis with experimental results. Before you object, that's simply the clinical way to say very young people reacted differently when they saw something that didn't match their expectations.

In one experiment, toddlers were shown a clear tub containing the same number of black and white balls. Researchers tracking eye movements showed that the children paid much more attention to a person who pulled balls of only one color out of the tub than someone who removed an equal number of balls of each color. What astonished the scientists was how quickly the toddlers assessed the ratio of black and white balls in the tub and came to expect that the color of the balls should be equally distributed. Of course, the children didn't set their expectations based on a statistically significant sample of the colored balls. They likely based their expectations on the visual rhythm of the balls in the tub—something our optical processing system is quick to recognize.

Jokes about white men not being able to dance (or jump) because they got no rhythm notwithstanding, a sense of rhythm seems to be a basic human trait. I once heard a musician explain that wherever he went, regardless of language or culture, if he gave an audience a three-note pattern they could always supply the fourth, on the beat.

When we talk of rhythm, we think first of music—perhaps because the beat of the song and the beat of a heart are not too far removed. But nearly everything we experience over time has rhythm.

When we talk about rhythm in writing, pacing is likely the first thing that comes to mind. Pacing, or the speed at which the story unfolds, is a critical element of writing because messing it up, like losing the rhythm in music, compromises the story.

There is more, however, to rhythm than maintaining a narrative velocity. Like tension and release, a rhythm that mixes faster and slower is more interesting than only one or the other. Short sentences and clipped dialog read faster and imply action, whereas complex sentences in long paragraphs—where you linger lovingly over every detail—slow both the rate at which the story unfolds and the tempo at which the reader can turn the pages. Just as a story that's non-stop action wears you out, writing entirely in short or long sentences quickly grows tiresome.

You should also consider the structural rhythm of the novel. A book that switches from one view-point character to another with each chapter has a different feel than a book told from a single point of view for the first half and another view point for the second.

Timing is another dimension of rhythm that's even harder to characterize. You likely know people who can't tell a joke to save their souls. One theory of comedy is that you build your audience up to expect you'll turn right and then, at the last moment, you turn left. The critical element in that theory is the *at-the-last-moment* part. It's simply not funny if you turn too late or too soon.

The closer together the resolution of each story thread, the stronger and more satisfying the ending. Mary Robinette Kowal described a draft where the protagonists resolved their personal relationship in one chapter, prepared to confront the antagonist in the next, and had the final conflict in the third. Her readers were indifferent to the ending. Then she reworked the three chapters so that none of the threads were resolved until the third and reported that most readers were moved to tears. The important point is that the essence of the story didn't change, only the timing.

Rhythm is one of the subtle but deep dimensions that distinguish great novels from the merely good. But like other aspects of the art of the long form, it rings hollow if you apply it too consciously. Instead, you need to internalize long form rhythm by learning the rhythms that work in other long form works like symphonies, films, and novels.

EMPHASIS

Now that we've talked about variation and rhythm, we can look at how to use these long-form tools for emphasis.

Stories are models. Models have the property of not being a perfectly faithful representation of the original. This is a good thing. A map that represents the precise location of every pebble in a field would have to be as big as the field. Similarly, a story that faithfully represents every single, trivial thing a character does would be indescribably boring.

A large part of the art of the storyteller is choosing

the interesting bits and sequencing them into a narrative that evokes the times, places, and events without getting lost in the details. It's fundamentally no different than creating a model or map to express the most interesting aspects of another, more complex thing.

But how do you know what to select for your story?

Some things may be inherently interesting. But most of the elements of a story are interesting because the storyteller gives them emphasis.

ATTENTION BUDGETS

From retinal structures in our eyes that detect motion, through subliminal filters, to the seat of reason in our frontal lobes, our brains are designed to ignore most of the information flowing into them. Attention is our cognitive priority queue. To say that something caught our attention means that, at least for a moment, that thing was the most important element in our personal universe.

The act of selection—singling a particular person, place, or thing out from all the similar ones—creates emphasis by calling it to our attention. Similarly, dwelling upon something creates emphasis. Readers, for example, assume that the amount of text devoted to a subject indicates its importance. A common novice mistake is to give us a loving crafted description of a character, say, a waiter, who appears only once in the story.

Which brings us to:

REPETITION

An advertising rule-of-thumb is that a person must hear about something seven times before they'll take action.

Fiction doesn't have to be quite so repetitive to create emphasis.

That said, I'm a firm believer in the *Rule of Two*:

> If it's important enough to put it in the book, it—whatever it is—should appear at least twice.

Applied consistently, it's how you encourage your readers to pay attention.

But repetition, in the long form, is more than simply a tool for creating emphasis. In conjunction with variation, it enables you to explore a deeper issue: how does the significance of something evolve over time?

MOTIF

Watching **Star Wars** in 1977 (back in the Dark Ages, before it had Roman numerals and a subtitle), was an amazing experience—one that's hard to convey to younger people who were weaned on photo-realistic computer graphics.

But for me, listening to the Star Wars sound track album was an even more amazing experience: it was the first time I heard a story unfold in another dimension—one that shadowed the visual experience, complementing, enriching, and extending it. That was when I began to understand musical motifs.

A motif is a recurrent thematic element.

At an abstract level, a motif is simply the application of the principle that a well-developed context makes references meaningful. Put that way, it sounds pretty bland. But think of the times when, caught up in a story, a well-placed word or phrase triggered a cascade of associations and emotions.

In John Williams' score for **Star Wars** there are motifs—the main theme, the rebel fanfare, the imperial march, Leia's theme, etc.—that are strongly associated with certain story elements the first time we hear them. Thereafter, the themes are quoted in other, often more complex, music for sequences like space battles, where many story elements come together. The musical quotes remind us, in the shadow dimension, of what happened when we heard the theme before and what that means for the stakes now.

A PALETTE OF MOTIFS

At one point, I thought I'd figured out how to stir-fry: chop up a bunch of vegetables, perhaps some meat, run it through the wok, add a bit of soy sauce, and presto—except my stir-fry wasn't as good as the dishes in the Chinese restaurants. Then I noticed one key difference. The dishes in the restaurants had fewer ingredients than mine did. There was more flavor when fewer flavors competed with each other. Less really was more.

Artists have long known that a picture is more vibrant with a limited palette of colors. Similarly, a limited palette of motifs is much more effective in a long-form work because the thematic elements must recur. Mix in too many motifs and you'll wind up with bland stir-fry.

THEME

"Wait," you say. "Theme? What gives? We've talked about

motif, emphasis, rhythm, variation, tension and release, and trajectory. Isn't it all basically the same thing?"

Perhaps—if you step back far enough and squint.

Part of the power of the long form is that you can examine subtle differences whose real significance only becomes apparent over time.

But at a deeper level, the topical similarity of the sections in this discussion of the long form illustrates the notion of theme. That is, we're exploring the theme of the long form.

Some writers stumble when asked about the theme of their novel. They say it's simply a story—nothing hidden below the surface. Others take the question of theme as open season, with no boredom restrictions, to expound the dissertation embedded in their text. The truth, as always, lies between these extremes.

Every piece has a theme because story is a model and the author has chosen what to include. But no piece's theme is the definitive statement on the topic because story is a model and the author has chosen what to exclude.

Theme is simply the idea you examine from various angles in the course of your piece.

The various angles are the key difference between theme and other dimensions, like emphasis. If, for example, you have a character who loves his wife, his dog, his job, and orange soda, you have four angles from which to explore the theme of love (particularly if some of those angles are in conflict). On the other hand, a book about why my political philosophy is right and yours is wrong may have a theme in the abstract sense of repetition with variation, but fails the various angles test.

Another way to think of it is that theme is the heart of

the conversation you want to have with your readers: the ground that you'd like to explore together.

PERSISTENCE OF VISION

P.O.V.

For writers it means, "point of view."

For artists, particularly those who work in film, it means, "persistence of vision."

We often invoke persistence of vision to explain the fact that we see smooth motion when a projector shows a sequence of still images at a rate of more than sixteen frames a second. Psychologists and physiologists don't have much use for the theory, but there's artistic truth in the concept that's particularly relevant to the art of the long form.

Each time a story element appears in the narrative we get a mental image of that element. Those images persist, at least on a conceptual level, and blend together to give us a synthetic view of the element.

The remarkable thing, thanks to our ability to find patterns, is that our vision always includes more than we've been shown. Once we've seen enough of a character, we feel we know them because we believe we can predict what they will do and how they will react.

In this sense, a key difference between long and short narrative forms is in the number of elements for which we can form persisting visions. In terms of character, the short form is like an evening out; the long form is like a journey together.

The artistic effect of persistence of vision gives us two keys for success in the long form:

- The images must all contribute to a consistent picture.
- The implications in the collage of images must be congruent with the story.

CONSISTENT PICTURE

In cinematography, an abrupt change in the stream of images is a jump cut, which we interpret as a change in context. In narrative, an abrupt change in character sticks out as an error or cheap trick. For example, readers won't accept a character that's been consistently kind to animals suddenly deciding to kick a cat. If kicking the cat is an important story point, then we need to see indications that the character might do such a thing before they actually do it.

Maintaining the consistency of the story elements is one of the challenges of the long form. On the flip side, the long form affords many more opportunities to show different dimensions of an element, weaving those aspects together for the reader in a way that surprises and delights.

CONGRUENT STORY

Congruency is more subtle because it operates on the level of the readers' expectations that go beyond the specific images you've shown in the narrative. My wife almost threw a book across the room when hours after a character finds true happiness (and scant pages from the end) she's run over by a car. The twist was incongruent with her expectations, and she felt the author took the easy way out.

This is not to say that the story has to be obvious. Quite the opposite: done right, each twist and turn, whether character or plot, gives the reader a richer picture by showing all the images up to that point in a new light. The most artful narratives bring the reader to a conclusion that is surprising and yet inevitable.

SERIES

No discussion of the long-form would be complete without looking at series.

There are two kinds of series: the open-ended series, in which known characters have continuing adventures (e.g., **Nancy Drew**), and the finite series that tells a story larger than a single book (e.g., **Harry Potter**). Open-ended series are like episodic television and could, in principle, go on forever (which is why most open-ended series are owned by a publisher who brings in work-for-hire authors to produce new volumes). Finite series are extra-long-form narratives, generally the work of a single, acknowledged author, that build to a final culmination.

Done right, a finite series can be a rewarding experience. If each book contributes a new, enriching view of the story, we begin to feel at home in that universe. Done poorly, we feel like we're stuck on a roller coaster covering the same increasingly tedious ground.

Undertaking a series is challenging—and risky if you're unpublished (which is why the common advice is to sell the first book before you write the others).

If you think you'd like to write a series, ask yourself some questions:

- Do you have enough story for multiple books? Or do you simply want to keep playing in the same playground?

- How will you give readers more of what they want and still keep it fresh? Can you do it without simply recycling the first book?

- Are you holding back your best ideas for the end of the series? What's going to keep the middle of the series from feeling like filler?

- Will your characters continue to develop over the course of the entire series?

I've tried to make the case that the art of the long form is qualitatively different from the art of the short form. The same is true for the art of the series compared to the art of the novel, though the differences are more subtle.

Consider the problem of the promise made to the reader at the very beginning: not only must you sustainably deliver new and interesting material across multiple books, you've also got to satisfy reader's expectations across the entire narrative span. Time and again, a series was ruined for me when the author, perhaps because they'd grown bored or jaded, took what felt like an arbitrary turn at the end.

A novel is a significant undertaking. A series of novels kicks the undertaking up by an order of magnitude. Beyond art, it takes a tremendous amount of dedication to do a series well.

THE OBLIGATION OF TRANSFORMATION

Have you ever walked out of a movie wishing you could

get a refund—not of the money you paid for the ticket but of the two hours of your life now lost forever?

When you produce a long-form project for an audience, you have an obligation to deliver something that is worth their time: the longer the form, the greater the obligation.

To be worth the time it takes to read, a novel must do more than merely distract. Modern audiences can find plenty to distract them—in the conceptual equivalent of convenient, bit-sized pieces—on YouTube and its ilk. And the parade of dancing cats and groin shots doesn't demand any focus or commitment.

What do readers expect in return for their attention?

It's not enough that the story goes somewhere; it has to transform the reader in the process.

Transformation is an intimidating word because we tend to use it only in the context of sweeping change. But don't be put off: we're talking here of transformation with a small, 't.' Changing lives isn't the purpose of the long form—though it can happen. Rather, the art of the long form is most truly expressed when your audience leaves enriched by the experience.

It is no accident that many narratives fit the pattern of the hero's journey. The act of reading allows the reader to experience their own hero's journey: the story takes the reader from the world they knew before picking up the book, into the abyss and the epiphanies of the unknown where they gain secret knowledge, and finally brings them back to the known, transformed by the journey.

That said, please don't get yourself worked up with worry that your manuscript isn't sufficiently mystical. The key here isn't mysticism, it is experience. Go back to the books you like to re-read. What is it about those books that keeps you coming back? Congratulations, you've just identified the transformative elements that, if you emulate, will help you meet the obligation in your own work.

STRONG FINISH

We occasionally say, with a touch of nostalgia, that all good things must come to an end. But the way a thing comes to an end determines, to a large extent, how good the thing was.

The ending matters. Regardless of how beautiful the prose, how evocative the characters, or masterful the dialog, if a short story fails to deliver a satisfying ending, you feel cheated. Given the far greater investment of time required by the long form, readers expect a commensurate payoff.

The long form is the most powerful medium for strong, satisfying endings because it affords authors the time to develop multiple story strands, each significant in its own right, and then weave them together for a strong finish. All those strands also mean, if you're not careful, that you've got enough rope to hang yourself.

Finishing, however, is much more than the ending.

Of the few network sitcoms I've enjoyed, nearly every one of them stayed on the air for one or two seasons too many. In some cases the final season was so disappointing that it soured the entire series for me. The best programs delivered consistently until they came to a graceful and satisfactory ending. Similarly, in sports, the players generally considered to be great are the ones who were consistent performers.

A strong finish is the capstone of a consistently good performance. That's why world-class gymnasts are expected to make a perfect landing after perfectly executing everything else in their routine.

RETROSPECTIVE

I sure you've often heard hindsight is 20/20. It is so well-worn a saying that it's beginning to take on a negative connotation like arm-chair quarterbacking. It is unfortunate that looking back is falling out of favor because one of the most illuminating perspectives is retrospect.

The ultimately most powerful but least appreciated potential of the long form is what you come to understand some time after the strong finish. Only after enough time has passed for the experience to mellow and ripen can you appreciate the work's lasting effect. Only when you can step back and look at the book in the context of what came before and after can you assess its significance.

Of course, there's nothing you can do to guarantee your book will become a timeless classic—nor should that be your goal. The only thing within your power is to write to the very best of your abilities, using the art of the long form to produce a book that delivers value to your readers each time they come back to it.

* * *

I hope, at very least, I've convinced you that working in the long form is more than simply making the short form longer.

I also hope that in doing so I haven't left you feeling intimidated by the terminology. If the list seems daunting, think of the items simply as the facets of a jewel. And like that jewel, the essence of the art of the long form is to create a whole that is greater than the sum of its parts.

CHAPTER 9.

EDITING AND REVISING

It's difficult, of course, to be told that your child isn't the most perfect in the world. It's equally difficult to hear that your manuscript could be improved.

As with most difficult things, one tends to go through the five stages of grief:

- **Denial** – That's not a problem.
- **Anger** – They missed the point.
- **Bargaining** – If I made this small change, would that fix it?
- **Depression** – I can never give them what they want.
- **Acceptance** – Maybe I can if I work at it.

I had a hard time reaching the stage of acceptance with an editorial letter because I didn't understand. Oh, I understood the words in the letter and the concepts behind them, but I didn't understand how to make the suggested changes. I stewed about it for two days. And then, on the third morning, I woke up, reread the letter, and I understood. It felt like a miracle.

Writing is the process of encoding thoughts as marks on a page. Reading is the process of decoding those marks and turning them back into thoughts. There's plenty of room for error in both processes. Because of that, understanding the thoughts of another and how they apply to your own thoughts is hard work.

Fortunately, it's the perfect sort of work for your subconscience: the best way to understand criticism is to study it and then sleep on it, perhaps for several nights.

KILLING YOUR DARLINGS

There is a set of actors, among whom comedians like Robin Williams and Jim Carey figure prominently, who can do remarkable work if kept tightly under control but quickly become tedious if left to their own devices.

I think of such talents when I hear the advice that writers must, "kill your darlings."

It's easy to hear, "Kill your darlings," as, "Delete the parts you like best,"—implying you can only write things you don't particularly like.

A better way to say it might be, "If it's too precious to go, it probably should go."

But the best way to say it is, "Nothing in the story is off-limits. Everything is open to scrutiny." If a word, phrase, passage, scene, or character doesn't contribute to the story, it should go. The overall balance of the story is more important than any individual element.

Which brings us back to the comedians: they grow tedious when they eclipse the story and reduce it to an excuse for a performance. But when a good director keeps them under control and allows them free reign only when it serves the story, the result can be delightful. By the same token, you don't have to kill your darlings when they're serving the story—but if they call attention to themselves, "Get the rope!"

SCRUTINIZE OVERUSED WORDS

The words on the list that follows are ones that tend to creep into your writing and dilute the ideas you're trying to convey because you use them all the time in normal conversation. It's not that the words on the list should never be used, it's that they need to earn their place in your manuscript, just like any other word.

> a little, almost, any, began to, certainly, definitely, even, exactly, fairly, just, perhaps, probably, proceeded to, quite, rather, real, really, seem, slightly, so, some, somewhat, sort of, started to, such that, usually, very, which

For example, "almost," is occasionally useful to describe a degree of completion but it muddies the meaning when you use it to imply, "a little less than." The phrase, "... he said, almost too brightly," is problematic because by saying what it almost is you're not saying what it is.

Similarly, "began to," and, "started to," are occasionally useful when it's important to know that something happened at the moment of starting some action, as in, "he star

PART II.

VERISIMILITUDE

CHAPTER 10.

THE APPEARANCE OF TRUTH

"Truthiness," coined by Stephen Colbert, was named Word of the Year for 2005 by the American Dialect Society and for 2006 by Merriam-Webster. It's a particularly funny word given the cultural and political climate in which it was coined, but there's a perfectly good, albeit venerable, word whose original sense means the same thing: verisimilitude.

Verisimilitude is, "the state or quality of being verisimilar; the appearance of truth; probability; likelihood." (Webster 1886)

Having the appearance, but not the substance, of truth is generally not considered a good thing. Fiction, however, is an exception. When you're dealing in something that in absolute terms is a lie (because it never happened in the real world), verisimilitude is a virtue.

The essence of the art of verisimilitude is to understand and apply real-world patterns and structures in your stories. Even in a fantasy world you can't ignore basic laws of economics—like how much farm land and how many people it takes in a medieval economy to support a single knight—if you don't want to alienate readers.

WHY FICTION? TRUTH IN THE UNTRUE

There is no such thing as objective history. Every attempt to recapture the past is an interpretation in which some things are emphasized more than others. We build models for the same reason: to emphasize some aspects of the thing being modeled while ignoring others. Interpretations and models are a simplification of reality. Fiction is the literary equivalent of model making. Our stories can speak truth more clearly because they omit the confusing and distracting things that are part and parcel of everyday life.

The first fantasy book that captured my imagination was the last book in **The Chronicles of Narnia**. [1] I stumble upon **The Last Battle** in my elementary school library after exhausting their meager collection of books on World War II. The word, "battle," in the title may have been what caught my eye.

I was mesmerized by the apocalyptic themes—it was easy to entertain apocalyptic notions during a time when everyone assumed nuclear war was inevitable—and enthralled by the conceptual scope of the fantasy. I found the theme of ever expanding vistas of worlds wider and richer than the one we know to be particularly compelling.

The transcendental surrealism (not a term I had in my grade-school lexicon) of the story was far more effective than a mind-expanding drug. I got my first taste of the way in which one could understand something more deeply and vibrantly if they were unencumbered by the constraints of ordinary experience.

Contrary to the common sense notion that the further a story strays from the real world the less relevant it is, fantasy enables us to abstract away ambiguity and tell a clearer and more compelling story about underlying truths. An interspecies war between orcs and elves is much easier to understand than a conflict between competing human ideologies and economic interests in the real world.

To be clear, I'm not arguing that fantastic stories are better than more realistic ones: any kind of story can convey truth. One of the basic rules of writing is, "show, don't tell." It's also a fundamental rule for life: people are much more willing to adopt an idea if you show them how to arrive at the notion themselves than if you hand it to them finished, polished, and ready to be placed on their mantle. A story can be spun that shows how concepts affect the lives of your characters much more clearly than trying to find an example in the life of an actual person.

So, why do we tell stories, particularly ones that aren't true?

Because like the jester, who is the only one in the court that can speak the truth, sometimes the untrue is truer than the true.

THE TRUE CORE OF A STORY

Why worry about truth in a book about creating the appearance of truth in fiction?

Because stories, like the best lies, are founded on truth.

You may feel overwhelmed with all this talk of truth, particularly if your aim is to entertain, not discourse on universal truth.

The true core at the heart of every good story is

something much closer to internal consistency than moral certitude.

I had a peculiar experience reading a trendy dystopian young adult novel: I didn't like the beginning, I liked the middle, and I didn't like the end. The first act seemed like a parade of contrivances to withhold information from both the protagonist and the reader. In the second act, when the protagonist finally gets some information and acts on it, I became engaged because I wanted to see how the experiment played out and what information that gave us for subsequent efforts to solve the problem. Then in the third act, through a series of startling reveals, I was effectively told everything I thought I knew about the story was wrong, there was no way I could figure out what was really going on, and so the only thing I could do was hang on for the wild ride to the end.

The novel had no true foundation. Except for the middle, the author didn't show me how to enjoy his story, he told me how to appreciate his cleverness as the designer and operator of a narrative roller coaster.

So what does this mean if you want engaged readers?

The first key to verisimilitude is that reading is interactive; your readers want to participate in the story. The best way to alienate them is to say, in effect, "Shut up, sit still, and let me take you for a ride." Engaged readers are ones who think about the book both while they read and after they stop. The best way to engage them is to establish the consistent foundation—the core truth—upon which the story plays out and because of which, when the tale ends, the reader will agree, even if it was a surprise, that the conclusion was inevitable.

A satisfied reader is the first, and most important, hallmark of verisimilitude in fiction.

* * *

This volume aims to help you better satisfy your readers.

Chapter two begins with a readers' Bill of Rights, courtesy of Mark Twain and Kurt Vonnegut, because the overall way in which you go about spinning your story determines whether your book rings true with readers. Chapter three explores the verisimilitude that arises naturally when thinking readers engage your story. Verisimilitude is the illusion of truth. We consider techniques that conjure or dispel those illusions in chapter four and in chapter 5 we look at competent wordsmithing, specifically those verbal non-sequiturs, awkward expressions, and linguistic gaffes that jar readers out of the story and break the illusion. Conflict that rings true is the dynamic key to verisimilitude. Chapter six wrestles the subject to the ground. In chapter seven, we look at the ways in which flubbing the details scuttles the verisimilitude of your story. Chapter eight continues the theme of enhancing verisimilitude by showing how to get major elements like action, societies, economies, magic, and science right. Writing intentionally, whether you prefer to outline or discover the story as you go, is the capstone of verisimilitude. Chapter nine looks at the preparation and research necessary to give your readers the illusion that you know what you're talking about. Finally, the appendix describes some story development tools that may help you improve the verisimilitude of your book.

CHAPTER 11.

A READER'S BILL OF RIGHTS

Before a reader can appreciate the verisimilitude of your story, they need to appreciate your book. They need enough evidence to trust that reading your book won't be a colossal waste of time. Readers are willing to give you the benefit of the doubt for roughly the first 50 pages to see if you seem to know what you're doing—that you can tell an intelligible tale about interesting characters—and that the story you promise to deliver meets their expectations.

Say, "meeting readers' expectations," and some writers bristle with indignation. They see themselves as producing art, not pandering to the mass market. The expectations outlined in this chapter, however, have nothing to do with the kind of story you tell: what really matters is how you tell it.

MARK TWAIN'S TEN RULES OF WRITING

Mark Twain set down his ten rules for writing, in part, because he believed James Fenimore Cooper broke them all. [2] I recommend these rules, not on Mark Twain's authority as a great writer, but on Samuel Clemens's ability to understand and articulate what frustrates readers.

LARGE RULES

- A tale shall accomplish something and arrive somewhere.

- The episodes of a tale shall be necessary parts of the tale, and shall help develop it.

- The personages in a tale shall be alive, except in the case of corpses, and that always the reader shall be able to tell the corpses from the others.

- The personages in a tale, both dead and alive, shall exhibit a sufficient excuse for being there.

- When the personages of a tale deal in conversation, the talk shall sound like human talk, and be talk such as human beings would be likely to talk in the given circumstances, and have a discoverable meaning, also a discoverable purpose, and a show of relevancy, and remain in the neighborhood of the subject in hand, and be interesting to the reader, and help out the tale, and stop when the people cannot think of anything more to say.

- The personages of a tale shall confine themselves to possibilities and let miracles alone; or, if they venture a miracle, the author must so plausibly set it forth as to make it look possible and reasonable.

LITTLE RULES

- An author should say what he is proposing to say, not merely come near it.
- Use the right word, not its second cousin.
- Eschew surplusage.
- Not omit necessary details.

KURT VONNEGUT'S EIGHT RULES OF WRITING

In his book, **Bagombo Snuff Box**, an assortment of short stories published in 1999, Vonnegut listed eight rules for writing a short story [3]:

1. Use the time of a total stranger in such a way that he or she will not feel the time was wasted.
2. Give the reader at least one character he or she can root for.
3. Every character should want something, even if it is only a glass of water.
4. Every sentence must do one of two things-reveal character or advance the action.
5. Start as close to the end as possible.
6. Be a Sadist. No matter how sweet and innocent your leading characters, make awful things happen to them—in order that the reader may see what they are made of.
7. Write to please just one person. If you open a window and make love to the world, so to speak, your story will get pneumonia.
8. Give your readers as much information as possible as soon as possible. To hell with suspense. Readers

should have such complete understanding of what is going on, where and why, that they could finish the story themselves, should cockroaches eat the last few pages.

* * *

I found the two sets of rules remarkable. Though separated by more than a century, both writers emphasize the one universal reader expectation: that they should be able to understand story.

Readers read because they want to immerse themselves in the story. In recent studies, brain scans of readers found the descriptions of touch, smell, and taste would light up the same cerebral regions as actual sensory stimulation. But readers can't immerse themselves in a story that doesn't make sense.

Narrative clarity is the second key to verisimilitude.

CHAPTER 12.

ENGAGING READERS

Roller coasters can be loads of fun (if you ignore the fact that you're simply going round in circles and that the ride is exactly the same every time) because you can pretend you're doing something dangerous while knowing that the engineers have done everything humanly possible to make sure the ride is safe. You must take care, however, to keep your roller coasters in the amusement parks, where they belong. Don't let them sneak into your plot.

"Wait," you object, "roller coasters are exciting. Don't we want our books to be equally exciting?"

Yes and no.

Clearly, if your story doesn't offer an experience that is compelling or enticing, few people will give you their money and invest their time to read. On the other hand, if your characters have as much influence on the course of events in your book as the riders on a roller coaster have on the direction in which they travel, you have an itinerary not a story.

Story is about cause and effect. We love good stories because we learn something about solving our own problems by going along with the characters as they try to solve theirs. A roller coaster story teaches us nothing more than, "Sit down, hang on, and enjoy the ride."

You don't have a real character unless they have two real choices and the ability to go either way. And you don't have a real story without at least two possible outcomes in play. The question of who will prevail must be open until the very end.

This is why you'll often hear people characterize the three act structure in terms of try-fail cycles. In act one, the protagonist tries something that fails to solve the story problem. They try something different in act two, which also fails. It's only in act three, where we're afraid the protagonist is about to get his or her third strike, that they succeed.

Of course, in a broader sense, every story is like a roller coaster because every time you read, the story takes you to the same place. The difference is that while we can see the tracks under the roller coaster, the story's tracks can disappear beneath the interplay of cause and effect, the verisimilitude of characters that have real choices, and situations that feel as though they could go either way.

The reason the tracks can disappear as the story unfolds for your readers is because they take an active part in it. Even if they know the story beforehand, the process of reading allows them to engage the context, characters, and concepts.

READERS ARE PARTICIPANTS NOT SUBJECTS

Boring a reader by not engaging them is bad enough. But letting a reader get engaged and then invalidating their efforts with a sudden twist borders on the criminal.

You may object that such things happen regularly in the movies.

But a book isn't a movie: readers must do the work both to visualize and to experience the story. And it is through that work that reading produces its unique pleasure.

Agent Jon Sternfeld explained the kind of engagement he looks for in books:

> "What 'engage' means here … is give your reader something to do. Readers are not passive vessels looking to be dragged somewhere and told a story. They're looking to get involved in a story—caring about the protagonist, wrestling with any issues that the narrative brings up, and most importantly, guessing what happens.… Readers want to take what is there on the page and extrapolate, use their imagination, draw conclusions, make assumptions. It's why they're reading a book and not watching a movie." [4]

Boring a reader by not engaging them is bad enough. But letting a reader get engaged and then invalidating their efforts with a sudden twist borders on the criminal.

You may object that such things happen regularly in the movies.

But a book isn't a movie: readers must do the work both to visualize and to experience the story.

It all comes down to respect: crafting your story so that it is, in effect, a conversation with your reader is the best way to steer clear of the roller coaster.

SOMETHING TO THINK ABOUT

As a reader, I most enjoy the books that give me plenty

to think about when I'm not reading. This means I need enough information to speculate about what's going on in the story and what might happen next.

Of course, we don't want to bring the story to a halt with a physics lecture or a history lesson. A skillful writer will weave all the key information the reader needs into the story.

There are actually two critical skills implied by that last sentence:

1. Being able to weave information into a story without breaking up its flow
2. Developing a sense of the information the reader actually needs.

For example, most readers will accept silicon rock creatures without worrying about their origins if the writer says they exist in the world of the story. In the middle of the book, readers would only care about the evolutionary biology of the silicon rock creatures if that information is the key to defeating them. But after they've read the book and want supplementary material, they may want to dive into speculative ecology.

LEARNING CURVES

I once heard an author of epic fantasy say that writers should give their readers, "a gentle learning curve." The point he was trying to make was that being able to ease your reader into the world of the book is an important skill.

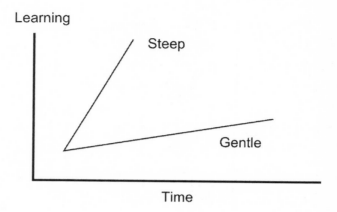

Many people, not just writers, misunderstand the concept of a learning curve. In a graph that shows learning (on the vertical axis) over time (on the horizontal axis), a gentle curve actually means that it takes the subject a long time to learn a little. A steep curve, by contrast, means that the subject quickly acquires the knowledge and information they need.

As with many things, however, when we examine the notion of learning curves more carefully, we find that for both different kinds of stories and different aspects of stories we want different kinds of learning curves. Fantastic stories need fairly steep learning curves so that the reader can understand the world. Contemporary or paranormal stories, on the other hand, only need gentle learning curves because they're not too different from the world with which the reader is already familiar.

Within a particular novel, the backstory should have a gentle learning curve. That is, a reader should be given a little at a time instead of a big info-dump. On the other hand, the basic information about setting, character, and plot should have a steep learning curve so that the reader is grounded and oriented in the story as quickly as possible.

* * *

Inviting readers to engage your story, by skillfully giving them open-ended information about characters and events as the narrative unfolds, dramatically improves its verisimilitude. It is, of course, consistent with how the world works—we are all intimately engaged with our lives and their attendant problems even though we don't understand everything that's going on.

But the real reason engagement increases verisimilitude is because engaged readers are busy filling in all the missing details based on their own experience. The story naturally rings more true to an engaged reader.

CHAPTER 13.

CREATING THE ILLUSION

There was a time when carrying a clipboard in public place implied you were acting in an official capacity—all the more so if you consulted the clipboard regularly and periodically made annotations. On a number of occasions (some purposeful and some not), I've been approached, while in public with a clipboard, by people who needed directions or assistance and assumed I could help them.

But if you try something similar now, you'll most likely be ignored. If you use a clipboard, the anachronism gives you away because everyone now expects that anyone official will use an electronic device. And if you try it with an appropriate device, you'll be ignored because everyone has their own devices. To paraphrase Syndrome, from **The Incredibles**, now that everyone has personal data capture devices, no one is special.

The rising, digitally-augmented generation will likely never appreciate the power of a clipboard. It's too bad because the illusion of expertise created by the clipboard is a perfect metaphor for verisimilitude in fiction.

Consider the similarity between the words *author* and

authority. Your aim is not to become an expert but an authority: you want your readers to believe you know what you're doing.

GOOD WRITING SEEMS EFFORTLESS AND INVISIBLE

The hallmark of an expert, regardless of their field, is that they make their efforts look effortless. You'll never achieve any measurable verisimilitude in your stories until you've mastered the art and craft of good writing. Like the puppeteer who makes the audience forget the strings and the person pulling them, your writing needs to be smooth enough that your readers forget the story has an author. If the readers see your hand in the story, you've broken the spell and ruined their illusion.

The number of ways you can spoil the illusion is legion. Beyond the obvious ones such as clumsy or overwrought writing, a host of subtle traps fall under the general rubric of being too clever.

CLEVER REFERENCES

There was a study claiming modern children are smarter, or at least more sophisticated, than their ancestors because of sitcoms. The study tracked the number of references to things, ideas, or events outside of the immediate story in each episode. They found that number increased over the last few decades. In other words, what the average viewer was expected to understand moved in the direction of more and briefer references to a broader range of common knowledge.

Working references to popular culture into your books is tempting because it shows how clever you are. But it's difficult enough to do well that you should almost always avoid the temptation.

First, there's the practical matter that clever references date your story.

Second, and more importantly, references to popular culture will almost always pull your reader out of the story, either to shake their heads if it's clumsy or in admiration if it's clever.

Consider the following lines from Phillip Reeve's **Starcross**. Together with **Larklight** and **Mothstorm**, the three middle-grade books tell rollicking tales of daring-do in the aether-ways of the solar system in a steampunk universe where Isaac Newton's discovery of the alchemical secrets of spaceflight propelled the British Empire out among the planets. In that world, the American Revolution was only the American Rebellion (thanks to the Royal Navy's aether ships). In the midst of a series of adventures, a French agent, who has just revealed her plans to relaunch the Liberty (the one American aether ship that survived the rebellion) says:

> "My grandfather hoped that he might capture a British warship or two, and set up a free American settlement upon one of the outer worlds … He dreamed of founding a Rebel Alliance which would strike at your empire from a hidden base …"

This is perhaps the best embedded reference to popular culture I've ever read. Every single word in the sentence is completely consistent with and fully motivated by the story. It's beautiful because it works on so many levels.

And yet when I read it, I dropped right out of the story in admiration.

THE LESSONS OF HOME VIDEO

Have you ever been subjected to the exquisite torture of watching unedited home video? There's nothing like sitting through half an hour of junior about to take his first bite of solid food to make you seriously entertain the notion of gnawing off your own arm to escape.

The problem with unedited home video is that years of viewing television and movies has lead us to believe that we should only have to watch the interesting bits.

This lesson applies equally to prose, though we usually talk about it in terms of moving the plot forward. That is, readers expect everything in the book to move the story forward. They assume authors aren't wasting their time with extraneous details.

Though it may seem counter-intuitive, one of the best ways to create the illusion of truth in fiction is to show less. I've shown friends and relatives—all of whom participated in the actual event—edited video that captured key moments and evoked the time and place, and they invariably say it looks better than they remembered.

Readers judge the verisimilitude of a piece by how well it matches their experience of reality. By showing only the scenes that convey something about the characters while moving the plot forward, they're left to fill in all the details and interstitial action themselves. The only source upon which they can draw for this material is their own experience with reality. That's why less feels more real.

But don't make the mistake of going too far.

WHEN ADDING MORE MAKES THE STORY SIMPLER

I'm a barely competent juggler. One of the things that surprised me on my short road to minimal mastery is that it's much easier to juggle three balls than it is to juggle two.

In a similar vein, sometimes having more story elements in motion simplifies the task of writing a scene or sequence. Perhaps it's only because the reader doesn't expect as much development with multiple elements, but it is often easier to show the story by juxtaposing several elements (e.g., actions, emotions, and concepts). Like video, where short scenes with cutaways are more interesting than long, static shots, having multiple elements means you can convey more with less by showing different facets of the subject.

Adding elements (within reason, of course) can also help increase the stakes in the narrative. For example, it's alarming if the hero is confronted by a gun-wielding killer, but it's more alarming if the hero, who is afraid of heights, is confronted by the gunman on top of a building.

And how should you handle the scenes you do show?

IN LATE, OUT EARLY

Stories should skip the boring bits. Why slog through the dull set-up and waiting when you can jump in right at the point where things get interesting? By the same token, why hang around after the action when you can jump away to the next interesting thing? One of the reasons readers keep reading is because they trust that you will not bore them with dull stuff.

But in-late/out-early is more than simply a way to keep your reader hooked. Once you develop a masterful sense of just how long a scene needs to be, in-late/out-early evolves from a mere technique for eliminating the boring bits into a tool for directing reader's attention and encouraging their engagement by inviting them to fill in the blanks.

DIRECTING FOCUS

Like their visual counter parts, scene breaks and screen or page time tell the reader where to focus their attention. In a long scene, with characters coming and going while other things transpire in the background, readers can pay attention to many things so no one thing will have their full attention. In a short scene, they can only pay attention to what you give them.

For example, let's say you have a scene where the main character notices another character acting strangely. If you show the main character strolling through the hall at school, greeting friends and chatting about the prom, until the boy she's had her eye on runs into them, nearly knocking her over while muttering something about the penguin revolution, and then the character and her friends spend a few more pages talking about what just happened and what it means for the prom, the reader may miss the key revelation about the penguin revolution. If, on the other hand, you jump into the scene moments before the collision and then jump out right after the first, "What was that?" comment, there's no danger of distracting the reader with the other people or the pending prom.

FILL IN THE BLANKS

However, the most subtle use of in-late/out-early—at a

level that approaches zen mastery—is to leave as much unsaid as possible.

Howard Tayler has often said, "The monster you imagine when I say something goes bump in the dark is far scarier than anything I could describe."

By showing only the most critical part of the scene, we allow readers to fill in the blanks and imagine what happened before and after the scene. In so doing, readers create a far richer experience for themselves than you as the author could by describing it all for them.

SUSPENSE

The last element necessary to create the illusion of truth in fiction is a purposeful distortion of reality. Readers want to be pulled through the story by their concern for the characters. The more they feel compelled to keep turning the pages, the greater the degree of verisimilitude they experience. And they're propelled onward through the story by suspense.

Suspense is … wait for it … is … waiting for it—but only in the simplest sense. While suspense may be characterized as the interval between a want and its gratification, delay is not, by itself, suspenseful. Standing in line at the checkout could be suspenseful if you desperately need to be elsewhere but usually it's simply tedious.

Similarly, uncertainty is an important element of suspense, but it's also insufficient to create suspense by itself. Hiding things from your reader in the name of suspense is a sure-fire recipe for reader frustration because they will either see through your evasiveness—questioning your abilities as a storyteller—or build up expectations your big twist will be hard pressed to fulfill.

It is a mistake to think that if a little delay or uncertainty is suspenseful, more delays or additional uncertainties will ratchet up the suspense meter. Actually, the more specific the uncertainty, the greater the suspense. Knowing exactly what will happen, but not when, is far more suspenseful than knowing the bad guys might be plotting something. By the same token, knowing when the bomb will go off and worrying whether the heroes can clear the area or defuse the bomb in time is much more suspenseful than knowing southern California will suffer a major earthquake someday.

Delays and uncertainties are suspenseful only if we care about the characters, their aims, and what's at risk should they fail. Worry, not just about what might happen but about what the characters might do next, is the high-octane fuel of suspense.

This is why it's nearly impossible to bring a reader to a high level of suspense in the first chapter: readers need time to empathize and identify with the characters before they're ready to worry about them. Suspense must be developed over time.

The key to developing suspense is to ratchet it up as the story unfolds. Readers either tire or grow accustomed to a constant level of suspense. Like the fisherman who alternately reels in and plays out the line, a series of tension and release cycles builds suspense by establishing patterns, increasing empathy, and believably raising the stakes.

There's an old story about a man whose upstairs neighbor would drop first one shoe and then the other each night when he went to bed. One night the man heard only one shoe drop and worked himself into a frenzy alternately waiting for the second shoe and worrying about what might have happened to the neighbor. Like jokes that depend on establishing a pattern that the punch line breaks, suspense grows when you play upon readers' expectations about patterns of tension and release.

Beyond simply varying the level of intensity in the narrative, cycles of tension and release help readers identify more strongly with and care more deeply about characters. A truism in romance is that couples who have shared a difficult experience are more likely to fall in love. One of the reasons, of course, is that the experience reveals something about the potential partner's character. But at a more visceral level the tension of the shared struggle and the release of the we-did-it! moment build empathy and identification. As with lovers, so too with readers and the characters they care about.

In the fishing analogy, the fisherman never plays out as much line as he reels in: at the end of each tension and release cycle, the fish is always a bit closer to the boat. The reader's sense of suspense will wither if each cycle of tension and release doesn't ratchet up their worry meter. If the characters solve some but not all the problems with which they're confronted during each tension-building episode, the reader will continue to worry about the unfinished business even as new challenges arise. In the climax, throwing a bigger version of a problem the characters were unable to handle earlier is a natural way to dial up the suspense.

With all of this, it's important to remember to use a light touch and leave as much unsaid as you can without confusing the reader.

CHAPTER 14.

COMPETENT WORDSMITHING

The one thing an illusionist must always do is avoid anything that breaks the spell. Like a Hollywood set, it doesn't matter if there's nothing behind the wall as long as the audience believes it's part of a much grander structure.

Eric Cummings said, "there's one basic, iron-clad, always-applicable rule of writing: say what you mean and mean what you say." In one of his first writing classes he thought he had a fairly good story, so he was surprised when the teacher read the first line and then stopped. His first line was, "Morning light barely flooded the room." The teacher asked, "What do you mean, 'barely flooded?'" [5]

Barely flooded— the words fight each other: to flood means, "an abundant flow or outpouring," so how do you barely have an abundant flow or outpouring? The senses of the two words are so different that the thing described can only be one or the other. It's the literary equivalent of garlic ice cream: it's hard to decide whether it's savory or sweet.

The problem with thoughtless constructions, like "barely flooded," is that they interrupt the reader's flow and force them to wonder how the author can have the story under control if he or she doesn't know how to use the language. As Eric said, the one fundamental rule of writing is that we must use our words deliberately and be willing to take responsibility for each and every one of them.

Competent wordsmithing—taking responsibility by using words deliberately—contributes to the verisimilitude of your story. Incompetent wordsmithing destroys it.

SHOWING INVOLVES CHARACTER-DRIVEN SPECIFICITY

It is usually a good idea to favor specific nouns over general ones—to identify a robin instead of simply saying it was a bird. In your quest to be specific, however, remember that if some is good, more is not necessarily better. If you describe every detail in the scene or setting in minute, concrete detail, your story will grind to a halt and you stand a good chance of losing readers with anything less than a Herculean attention span. In general, a few specific, evocative details, leaving plenty of room for your reader to fill in the rest, work best.

But how do you choose which details to include? Because you're always writing from a point of view, choose the ones that tell the most about the character. A dentist, for example, who has shown no evidence of an interest in firearms wouldn't register the make and model of the gun a mugger was waving in his face but would probably notice the man's bad teeth.

TELLING DETAILS

We all know we're supposed to show not tell. Telling is stating that someone or something is a certain way, and expecting readers to simply believe us. Showing is about providing enough evidence for readers to come to the same conclusion on their own.

Of the two, telling is far more economical with words because we rely on shared understanding to fill in details. The problem with shared understanding is that there's a great deal of variation: saying a character is a grouch may conjure images of an irascible neighbor for one reader and puppet in a trash can for another. Worse, readers likely won't care if we simply assert a story is important. Reader involvement depends upon the readers finding their own reasons to care about the story.

That said, there is one kind of telling that is critical to get right if you want readers to embrace the story and to trust you as the storyteller: the telling detail.

A telling detail is a supporting element, mentioned in passing, that someone familiar with the setting, situation, or process would know. Whether it's the layout of the streets in a particular city, what it feels like to drive a car off a highway embankment, or the way police officers actually use guns, each time you get a telling detail right, you signal your readers that you actually know what you're talking about. Conversely, botching something that is well known or easy to check makes readers wary and suspicious. If you provide a few accurate telling details that match readers' knowledge and expectations, they'll happily trust you when you take them places beyond their experience.

The art of storytelling really comes down to choosing

what to show and what to tell. A telling detail helps the reader determine the context in which the story takes place without interrupting the action. And if the details are well-chosen, they will both vividly invoke the object or setting and increase your story's verisimilitude by suggesting you know what you're talking about.

Be sure, however, that you know what images and associations the details you choose to emphasize will evoke.

EXTRAORDINARY CHARACTERIZATION AND MUDDLED METAPHORS

In his book, **Stein on Writing**, Sol Stein said:

"... characterize by an action. We individualize by seeing characters doing things and saying things, not by the author telling us about them. Don't ever stop your story to characterize. Avoid telling the reader what your character is like. Let the reader see your characters talking and doing things." [6]

Stein outlines five ways to characterize:

- "Through physical attributes."
- "With clothing or the manner of wearing clothing."
- "Through psychological attributes and mannerisms."
- "Through actions."
- "In dialogue."

Stein is correct, but some of his examples of good characterization sound overwrought out of context. Worse, others mix or muddle metaphors. For example, instead of, "Ellen looked terrific in her gown," Stein suggests, "In her gown, Ellen looked like the stamen of a flower made of silk."

The stamen and the pistils of a flower (the spindly bits that stick out in the center) are the plant's reproductive structures—probably not the first part of the flower we visualize when we think of beauty. There's also the inconvenient fact that the stamen is the male part of the plant.

The essence of Stein's advice is that the world of our common experience is so common, so ordinary that only the uncommon and extraordinary serve to characterize. I agree. But be careful, when striving to capture the extraordinary, not to muddle metaphors—nothing squelches verisimilitude as quickly as trying too hard.

LINGUISTIC SPICES

Spices are an interesting sub category of food that, to the best of my knowledge, have the common property of a little working wonders in a dish but too much ruining everything.

I use the term, "linguistic spices," to cover all elements of language, idiom, and usage that might cause readers to stumble. Dialect, especially if it is transcribed faithfully, forces readers to sound out each word. Slang may be ambiguous or unfamiliar the farther removed your readers are in time and space from the people who originated the terms. Objectionable language, including profanity, may offend or annoy readers.

Used sparingly and purposefully, linguistic spices can

convey volumes. Consider a character established as proper throughout the story who loses his or her composure and swears at a critical moment. Or a villain, who when unmasked, chooses to show his contempt with contemptible language.

The analogy also applies in terms of tastes: young people are often not ready for spices. A good host should try to serve foods their guests will enjoy.

Of course, you don't have to clear out your spice rack because some of the items might not be appropriate for everyone's tastes. Doing so would be as limiting as adding cilantro to everything because it's the currently fashionable ingredient.

The attribute that should distinguish those of us who call ourselves writers from others who put words together is our ability to use language to achieve an intended effect. To that end we ought to master all the facets of our language so that we can write with intent and choose the right ingredient for the job from a full, rich palette.

SPEECH TAGS

Speech tags are one aspect of fiction where writers often undermine the verisimilitude of their story. Like highway markers that help maintain the orderly flow of traffic, speech tags should do nothing more than unobtrusively identify the speaker. Many writers, however, bolstered by a long string of published precedents, overload their speech tags, calling attention to their writing in a way that breaks up the flow of the story.

In ideal prose, the dialog is so distinct that the reader knows the identity of the speaker without any additional attribution. In practice, the ideal is rarely achieved and dialog requires attribution.

A MINIMAL SPEECH TAG FRAMEWORK

The reader must never be confused about who is speaking. The best way to assure clarity without interrupting the flow of the dialogue is to use a consistent pattern of attribution. You want your readers to register the identity of the speaker without noticing the speech tags.

ATTRIBUTION RULES

- Use, "said," and, "asked," primarily. An alternate tag might occasionally be warranted, but you'd better have a very good reason.

- Use the form "Fred said", not "said Fred." *Said* comes last with the prepositional form ("said he" sounds archaic). There's no reason not to be consistent (aside from the long fashion of using the said-first form).

- Only apply adverbs to the verb, "said," that qualify the physical act of speaking. You're telling the reader something about the way the character spoke if you say, "said loudly."

- Use beats to convey non-verbal communication and show the emotional state of the speaker. A beat is a sentence in the same paragraph as the dialog that describes what the speaker is doing or feeling.

- Omit speech tags when it's clear who is speaking. Use

tags or beats to identify the speakers periodically so that the reader doesn't lose track of speaker order.

- Use speech tags whenever speaker order changes. In general, you are only able to omit speech tags when two characters speak in alternating lines.

ADVERBS IN SPEECH TAGS

The job of an adverb is to modify a verb. Sometimes we need to qualify an action and we don't have a direct verb that does the job. Adverbs have their place so long as we use them sparingly.

We get in trouble, particularly in speech tags, when we confuse actions and intentions. For example, consider a medic working on a battlefield. Saying that the medic cut quickly or cut carefully qualifies the action and gives us, as readers, evidence to infer the medic's intent. On the other hand, saying he cut viciously qualifies the intent behind the action and not the action itself.

Resist using adverbs with speech tags because it's too easy to fall into the trap of qualifying intention (e.g., "he said disdainfully"): it's lazy writing because a character's intention should be conveyed explicitly through either dialog or description.

Similarly, you should always use a direct verb (e.g., shouted or called) instead of a qualified verb (e.g., said loudly) if the direct verb can do the job. Occasionally no direct verb has the right sense so you need to qualify the closest verb. For example, if you wanted to describe a character speaking to a group who raises his voice to make sure someone else in the room will hear, he's neither shouting nor calling, so, "said loudly," might be your best choice.

* * *

There are a great many other ways in which incompetent wordsmithing can spoil the illusion in fiction. And even if you take the utmost care, there will be readers who complain that something you did or didn't do ruined the book for them. You can't please everyone all of the time. But with reasonable care and practice, you can avoid the most obvious missteps that break the illusion and give your readers the pleasure of a story with a high degree of verisimilitude.

CHAPTER 15.

CONFLICT THAT RINGS TRUE

While we all hope for peace, so much of our existence is defined by conflict it is imperative you get it right if you want to deliver a compelling story.

DOES CONFLICT MEAN THAT SOMEONE'S MEAN?

I spoke with a writer who was concerned that she didn't have enough conflict and was afraid she couldn't fix it because she didn't like to write about mean people. I pointed out that because they've found ways to justify their actions, even the most hardened criminals don't believe themselves to be bad people.

Worrying, however, about whether people are good or bad, nice or mean, muddies the storytelling waters and actually introduces a subtle bit of moralizing.

How so?

Story and conflict arise from two simple questions:

- What does each character want?

- What are they each willing to do to get it?

If you have two characters who each want the same thing (a thing that only one of them can have) and who are both willing to go to great lengths to get it, you have automatic conflict.

And the beauty is that neither of them has to be mean. In fact if they're both driven by worthy motives you'll have a much better conflict than a simple good vs. bad scenario.

After all, the parents grappling in the stores for the last trendy toy are only in the melee because they want to do something nice for their kids.

INTERNAL CONFLICT: SINE QUA NON

There's an entire set of words and phrases which have come down to us from Latin that we're slowly losing because knowledge of ancient languages is no longer a hallmark of a good education. Even **Harry Potter** hasn't been able to resurrect more than a few spell phrases from that dead language.

It's unfortunate because some ideas are best expressed in other languages. For example, *sine qua non* is a Latin legal term that we must translate into the more awkward, "without which it could not be." *Sine qua non*, captures the notion of something so necessary it's definitional.

Internal conflict is the *sine qua non* of story.

Some of you, particularly if you equate internal conflict with navel gazing or whiny teenagers, may roll your eyes at that assertion. You may say, for example, that your story is about action and your characters neither want nor need to take time off from dodging bullets to inventory their feelings.

I understand your objection, but answer this question: what's the common wisdom about characters and flaws?

If you said something along the lines of flawed is good (i.e., relatable and interesting) and perfect is bad (i.e., boring or self-indulgent), you're in the right ballpark.

So why do we like flawed characters?

Is it because they allow us to feel superior?

No. It's simply that flaws produce internal conflict. That's what people really mean when they say they find flawed characters more compelling than perfect ones.

Internal conflict gives us greater insight into character. There's nothing to learn from a perfect character: if we can't compare and contrast the thought processes that early in the character's development lead to failure and later to success, we can't apply any lessons to our own behavior.

Internal conflict also creates a greater degree of verisimilitude (because who among us doesn't have a seething mass of contradictions swimming around in his or her brain case?).

Character flaws and their accompanying internal conflicts arise from uncertainty. If your characters are certain about how to resolve the problem, you have an instruction manual not a story.

Ergo, internal conflict is the *sine qua non* of story. Stories where conflicts at different levels reflect and reinforce each other are the most interesting because their mutual resolution can be the most satisfying.

ANTAGONISTS AND THE SOURCE OF CONFLICT

When we talk about the fundamentals of writing, we generally juxtapose protagonist and antagonist without any separate consideration of the source of conflict.

Because the antagonist is often the source of conflict, particularly in realistic stories, this gloss is fine. But other times, the antagonist is motivated to oppose the protagonist by an external source of conflict.

It helps to be clear on the distinction between the antagonist and the source of conflict, and to understand the structural implications for stories where they are one and the same, and stories where they are distinct.

The antagonist opposes the protagonist by acting against him or her. In order to show and understand the conflict that drives the story, the antagonist must be introduced at about the same time as the protagonist.

The source of conflict is the person or agency that causes the antagonist to act against the protagonist, either directly (e.g., the bad guy sends his henchmen), or indirectly by creating conditions that force the protagonist and the antagonist to compete (e.g., they must fight to the death in the arena).

For example, in a fairy tale, the minion sent out to slay the child of destiny and who repeatedly tries but fails during the course of the book is an antagonist, while the evil queen who sent the minion is the source of conflict. Often the climax includes the revelation that the minion, whom we thought was bad enough, is nothing compared to the queen.

You might argue that the source of conflict is the ultimate antagonist because many stories end only when the protagonist finally manages to destroy the source of conflict. If you want to think in terms of major and minor antagonists, that's fine.

But it's important to be clear on the distinction between the character who actively opposes your protagonists and the reason that character opposes the protagonist. The Emperor Palpatine was the ultimate source of conflict in **Star Wars**—and the story didn't end until he was destroyed—but it was Darth Vader who most actively opposed Luke and Han.

NON-CHARACTER ANTAGONISTS

What if your story doesn't have an actual antagonist character and instead conflict comes from within or without?

If you ask writers about kinds of stories you'll likely get a variation on the classic triumvirate of man vs. self, man vs. man, and man vs. nature. I like to add a few more gradations to the sources of conflict:

- **Self** – Internal demons, conflicting needs or desires, psychological dissonance
- **People** – Lovers, family, friends, and people with whom the protagonist has more than casual relationships
- **Society** – Organizations, clubs, cabals, conspiracies, churches, companies, bureaucracies, armies, parties, governments, movements, etc.
- **Nature** – A particular feature of the natural world: animals, mountains, oceans, storms, droughts, etc.
- **Universe/God** – The external world in general

What's convenient about having an antagonist as a character is that it's easier to give our protagonists the moral high ground if the conflict is forced upon them by someone.

Of course, some stories don't (or can't) embody the forces working against the protagonist in a single character. Showing multiple characters opposing the protagonist signals there are larger forces at work.

But there's a deeper reason that the conflict in the vast majority of stories occurs at the level of people and society: conflict is fundamentally interpersonal.

Before you accuse me of forgetting the question, let me explain: in the same vein as the philosophic question about trees falling in the forest, there are no stories about the world that existed before people. It's not that things didn't happen—indeed, if contemporary, computer animation-rich dinosaur documentaries are to be believed, there was plenty of red-in-tooth-and-claw conflict—it's that there was no one around to attribute significance to the actors and events. Was it good or bad that the tyrannosaurus took out the ailing duckbill?

Often, scarcity is the source of conflict. A great many sports, for example, depend on the fact that there are two teams and only one ball. But the significance of the conflict depends upon the meaning we assign to it.

"Okay," you say, "what about a man trying to conquer a mountain?"

It all depends on why he's trying to conquer the mountain. If he's trying to get to the other side to find the cure for the fever in his village, then it's a heroic conflict. If he's trying to get to the other side to enslave the village there, then it's a very different sort of conflict.

Put another way, regardless of the source of conflict, the first thing readers want to know is, "Why should we care?" Most people find it very difficult to care about anything they can't understand in personal terms. When another person or persons oppose the protagonist, readers immediately recognize the personal stakes. When the source of conflict is non-personal—either internal or external—you must show why that conflict matters to your protagonist and, by extension, your readers.

CHAPTER 16.

MAKE SURE THE NUMBERS ADD UP

One of the best ways to undermine the verisimilitude of your story is to throw around numbers that don't add up.

I ran into this problem in a high-profile book where the author characterized a safe zone in a strange setting as being, "several times the size of a football field," with livestock pens in one of the corners that held cows, pigs, and sheep—enough to make the community of about fifty self-sufficient.

Leaving aside the fact that sheep produce nothing the residents can use—there was no mention of any attempt to process the wool—until they're slaughtered and are thus a terrible choice for the constrained space of the safe zone, we're presented with several kinds of domesticated animals that require either a non-trivial amount of food, or abundant pasture.

Here's how the numbers break down:

- Cows generally require three to five acres each.
- There are 43,560 square feet in an acre.

- A regulation football field, with end zones and side lines is 120 x 60 yards, or 64,800 square feet.

- If several football fields means four, that's 259,200 square feet, or about 5.9 acres. Even if we're generous and assume it's twice the size, that's only 11.8 acres, or enough pasture for about four cows.

- But the safe zone is divided roughly into quarters, with a lot of paving. Moreover, the livestock quarter has barns and a slaughter house, further reducing its area.

The bottom line is that there's barely enough land to support one cow—which clearly isn't enough to sustain fifty people.

This may seem pedantic, but the fact that the numbers didn't add up yanked me out of the story and diminished my willingness to trust the author.

THE DEVIL IS IN THE DETAILS

One of the funniest moments in **Plan 9 from Outer Space** is when the zombies reanimated by the aliens march out of the graveyard, past tombstones that are obviously plywood cutouts because they wobble. [7] You may want to believe that your readers will be so swept away with the story they won't notice the fake tombstones but it didn't work for **Plan 9**, and it won't work for your thinking readers. Botching the details is a sure-fire way to reduce your literary classic to a laughable B-movie.

Of the many mistakes you can make, the one you must always avoid is underestimating your readers. Someone will check every fact and figure you use in your story—not because there's a secret Ministry of Truth in Literature out there but because readers are trying to map that information into their mental model of your story. What sets our species apart is our need to make sense of the world, which is why you can't toss out random stuff and expect your readers to be satisfied.

"But," you may say, "the world often doesn't make sense."

That's true, particularly of our social world—and a good thing too because if the world made sense we wouldn't need books to help us understand it.

Our physical world, however, is deeply regular and consistent: from the clockwork of seasons, tides, and days and nights, to the invariant laws of gravity, thermodynamics, and entropy, a given cause always produces the same effect. Because this is the substance of our daily experience, we expect the same from our literature.

The difference between a knock off and the real thing, whether we're talking art or brand-name products, is in the details and the quality of the relationships among the parts. Facts that fit together and numbers that add up are like the quality of the stitching you find on the seams inside your expensive designer hand bag.

So, the bad news is you can't achieve verisimilitude without doing your homework. The good news is that the homework is straightforward if you understand one principle: the cement of verisimilitude is reason. Every element in your story must have a reason for being there because as soon as the tombstones start wobbling you've lost your readers.

SETTING IS MORE THAN A STAGE

In the early 19th century the north-eastern U.S. was called, "the burned-over district," after a series of religious revivals left the people there tired of the whole business. In a similar vein, lots of paper has been devoted to tales of swords and sorcery—so much so that medieval settings are a kind of literary burned-over district.

Tolkien placed **The Lord of the Rings** in a medieval setting because he wanted a legendary, almost mythic feel. Since then, a great many other writers have gone over the same ground because they wanted a Tolkienesque feel.

Choosing a setting simply because that's what the cool kids do is a sure-fire way to undermine the verisimilitude of your story. If you can't taste the shifting scents in the air, hear the wind whispering through the trees or howling over the rocks, and repeat the secret names of the nineteen different kinds of snow, how will your readers get any more than a general sense of the place where your story unfolds?

Given a story you want to tell, why does it have to be in a particular place and time?

The question is important because the setting is really a meta-character. It requires the same care in avoiding stereotypes as any of your other characters. In particular, the setting needs more of a reason for being than because it provides a stage and props. If you can take your fantasy epic and turn it into a space opera by replacing magic with advanced technology, you should ask yourself some hard questions about your setting and whether it's pulling its weight in the story—because your readers will.

NO MONOCULTURES

One of the nice things about fantasy is that you can define away moral grey areas by making enemies a different species that is congenitally at war with the good guys. In **The Lord of the Rings**, for example, none of the fellowship gives a second thought to the morality of killing orcs. This advantage, however, can become a liability if you fall into the trap of creating monocultures.

The term, "monoculture," stems from the practice in industrial agricultural of growing vast fields of genetically identical plants. It's much easier to run a mechanized farm around a uniform crop, but you risk losing everything if a disease develops to which the plants are susceptible. Planting with a variety of seed may not yield as much under optimal conditions but the chance that some of your crop will survive in a bad year is much better. Indeed, agricultural scientists have begun to recognize the value of wild varieties because they serve as a genetic reservoir against ever more vigorous diseases.

As in agriculture, so too in fiction: it's easy to make all dwarfs dour and stolid, all elves ethereal, and all goblins bloodthirsty but you're practically guaranteed to fall victim to the verisimilitude-draining disease of stereotyping. In the worst cases, entire races have a single personality and you can't tell one individual from another.

Why does monoculture undermine verisimilitude?

Pick a group in the world around you. Do all adherents of a particular political party or faith act and think the same way? Their enemies think so, but if you've ever met more than a few of *those* people you know it's not true: not only do members differ in their individual personalities and qualities, but the very notion of membership is nebulous with people exhibiting different degrees of commitment to the cause.

Outside of special organizations, like the military, which go to great lengths to enforce uniformity, any time you have a group of people you'll have variety of appearances, attitudes, and approaches. In fact, it is the tension between conformity and conflict that is one of the primary drivers of social dynamics.

The good news is that monocultures are so prevalent in literature that a little effort to show variation among your characters is an easy way to boost the verisimilitude of your story.

WORLD-THREATENING STAKES

A writing friend asked, "Am I right in thinking that realistic fiction plots can be, 'I hope I get the cute guy,' 'I'm going to save my dad from this terrible disease,' etc. (i.e., major conflicts that we have in real life), but fantasy fiction plots have to involve the kingdom or the world?"

It's not that the stakes in fantasy must be world-threatening, but it's easier to make them so.

In the real world, nothing (except perhaps an errant asteroid or the sun exploding) threatens the entire planet; at worst there are threats to our personal or social worlds. In fantasy, the author can say the villain's Frog of Doom will swallow the planet if the hero doesn't stop him and we accept the threat because we accept the author's description of the fantastic world.

Of course, the world we know is only one of a universe of worlds that can be imperiled. Aprilynne Pike's **Wings**, for example, is mostly the story of the protagonist's discovery of her fairy heritage and a rather nasty run-in she has with some trolls. But the stakes go up with the revelation that she was placed in our world to guard a gateway to Fairy Land, which the trolls would dearly like to find and pull apart, petal by petal. [8]

Put another way, in fantasy it's easier to extrapolate the personal threats to a broader population and thus raise the stakes. If the villain can turn the hero into a warthog, what's to stop him from turning everyone else into warthogs?

Part of the reason we do this is because we all indulge a deep, common fantasy that we are significant in the larger scheme of things. We tend to bring out that theme, often as the *child of destiny*, because it's much harder to indulge that fantasy in the real world— which sometimes seems to go out of its way to prove otherwise.

Story problems that ring true are proportional to the characters. A threat that is too small is laughable while a threat that is too large becomes meaningless (if the world blows up, everything ceases to matter). The stakes that have the greatest degree of verisimilitude are tied to problems the protagonist has a chance of solving. This isn't to say that you can never have large-scale stakes—if the hero fails to stop the villain many people will suffer—but those stakes should flow naturally from the conflict.

PRACTICAL MAGIC

The key to verisimilitude is to give readers enough of the appearance of truth in your story that they are willing to suspend their disbelief.

Howard Tayler is fond of saying, "Explain the heck out of something small, then wave your hands over the big things." In other words, show readers you know that you're talking about in one case, which they can verify, and they're generally willing to believe what you say about other cases. If, however, you mess up the simple details, readers have reason to doubt everything else you tell them.

The details you have to get right depend on the particular story you wish to tell. But you can start out on the right foot if you avoid the common traps of a setting that's nothing more than a back drop, monocultural characters, and disproportionate stakes. In all these cases, the best way to improve your verisimilitude is to show diversity and make sure the numbers add up.

CHAPTER 17.

GETTING THINGS RIGHT

I once took a course whose subtitle was, "The future isn't what it used to be." We studied a historiography of people writing about the city of the future. With the professor's guidance, we observed that in virtually all the visions of the world of tomorrow there was no evidence of the past: not a single decrepit or historic building sullied the prospect of the gleaming tomorrow-land enjoyed by its residents from their flying cars.

I found it uncanny, like the latest Japanese androids that look almost but not quite human. Without historic reference points, I couldn't place those cities with respect to the world I knew. Was the architectural fantasy of domes and monorails decades or millennia away?

The world in which we live is the product of processes acting over time. From the broad sweep of geology and evolution to the conscious and unconscious effects of people living their lives, the present is an amalgam of the past.

When asked for his advice on world-building, Scott

Westerfeld said, "Pay attention to how this world works, and how complicated it is."

Much of that complexity arises around points of contact where different forces, be they natural or social, collide. Add the dynamics of ebb and flow to the colliding forces and you have the natural recipe for a complex web of competing interests that rings true. Think of the intertidal zone, alternately flooded and exposed, and the profusion of life you find there.

In contrast, particularly among those of us who tell fantastic stories, the setting often becomes simply the ground on which we compete for the most outlandish vision. Without any thought to the processes and forces that could have given rise to such a thing, we're playing the same uncanny game as the architects of the City of the Future.

The best way to ratchet up the verisimilitude of your world is to give it a history and fill it with evidence of the past. You don't need to turn your fantasy adventure into a textbook, but if you show your readers evidence of things in your world that have changed over time, they'll be willing to believe that, like our own, your world has been around long enough to feel real.

GETTING ACTION SEQUENCES RIGHT

Action is best understood as the movement and collision of opposing forces. There's rhythm, pacing, and a certain inexorability to the action sequence—if not, the characters could simply side-step the unpleasant consequences.

Most people don't realize how quickly real action happens—that there's a lot of waiting, a moment of chaos, and grim work afterward to deal with the consequences. War is 99% boredom and 1% terror.

Big action is made up of a great many smaller actions. For example, J. Michael Straczynski once outlined the logic of a space battle between the Narns and the Shadows in **Babylon 5**. He broke the action down into the following phases:

- Detection
- Deploy long-range weapons
- Close to effective range
- Major and minor encounters
- Break off or destruction
- Aftermath

By the same token, fist fights and small gun battles have structure. You don't simply run out, exposing yourself to attack, and start pummeling your opponent. Instead, you size them up, looking for a weakness to exploit.

It's tempting to think about cool action—guys flying through the air, things exploding, etc.—but eye candy, whether in print or on the screen quickly grows tiresome it if doesn't arise from an inevitable underlying structural logic.

GETTING DYSTOPIAN SOCIETIES RIGHT

In the current bumper crop of young adult dystopian offerings, the societies in which the stories take place tend to cluster around the ends of the spectrum between order and chaos.

At one level, this clustering is simply classic extrapolation: taking an aspect of current society, amplifying it, and working out its ramifications. But at another level, we're in the midst of creating dystopian tropes and, soon, clichés, because some authors commit a sin with their society that they would never commit with their antagonists: stereotyping.

There's no room in modern literature for characters that are purely good or evil. Characters, at least ones who ring true, are more complex. The best villains sincerely believe they are the heroes of their own story and that the fruit of their labors will be a better world.

So how do you avoid stereotypes, like an oppressive government, when developing your dystopian society?

Socrates set the precedent when, in **The Republic**, he suggested the way to understand personal virtue was to examine virtue on the scale of a state. [9] In other words, approach your dystopian society just as you would a character—specifically, your antagonist.

Like good characters, societies need back stories that outline a plausible path to the present. People don't wake up one day and decide to be evil. Similarly, whole societies don't turn to oppression overnight.

The proper study of how societies change over time keeps an army of sociologists, anthropologist, and historians busy. We can't begin to do justice to such a rich field of inquiry here, but one key to creating believable dystopian societies is to remember that there are always winners and losers: one person's dystopia is another's utopia.

The real engine of any society is the much larger group

in the middle: people who are neither the winners nor the losers, but buy into the system because they hope to become winners. During the U.S. Civil War, for example, most of the men fighting for the South were not slaveholders and, in strict economic terms, were not able to compete with the labor advantages enjoyed by the plantations in the peculiar institution for which they were prepared to die.

The good news is that a dystopian society showing the lengths to which reasonable people can go in supporting an increasingly irrational social system is far more frightening than one that's bad simply because it's bad.

GETTING ECONOMIES RIGHT

I've enjoyed Harry Potter along with a substantial number of the other residents of this planet. And I've dutifully paid my Potter-tax by purchasing both the books and the movies. However, part way through I found that I enjoyed J.K. Rowling's mix of magic and muggles more if I thought about it less.

To say that parts of the wizarding world don't quite ring true is laughably like straining at a gnat and swallowing a camel because, in an objective sense, none of it rings true.

So, what's my problem?

The apparent absence of a wizard economy.

Yes, we see commerce in Diagon Alley, and you need wizard gold to purchase sweets on the Hogwarts Express. But aside from the obvious parallels to the economic disparities in the world of our ordinary experience (i.e., wizard who aren't independently wealthy have jobs—apparently all at the Ministry of Magic) we don't see the wizard economy in action. And because the ability to do magic appears to be wholly unrelated to the size of one's account at Gringott's, we don't get anything more than an anecdotal sense from the Malfoys and Weasleys of what it means for witches and wizards to be rich or poor.

Of course, Rowling never set out to do an economic study. And a staggering number of people have enjoyed the stories as they stand. Nonetheless, a little more attention to these questions could have improved the verisimilitude of the stories.

Why?

Because knowing what things cost helps increase the tension and ratchet up the stakes.

How, then, do you get economies right?

Economies are networks in which actors take inputs and transform them into higher-value outputs they can exchange with other actors. A trader, for example, buys low at the source and adds value by transporting the goods to a market where relative scarcity allows him or her to sell high. In Harry Potter, where magical folk can conjure much of what they want, there's little need for economic networks.

There's also the matter of economic scope. If, in your medieval fantasy, you want two armies of 10,000 knights each to meet in battle, to paraphrase Ricky Ricardo, "you've got some 'splaining to do." During the medieval era in our world, it took twelve hundred acres—roughly two square miles—of cultivated land to support a single armored knight. If the land was uniformly fertile, you would need an area the size of the state of Maryland to support one army of 10,000 knights. It would be difficult to maintain political cohesion (i.e., to keep all 10,000 knights from fighting among themselves) over that much territory with a standard feudal organization. In other words, if your story runs afoul of economics as we understand it in our world, you're going to have to take the time to establish how it works in your world.

If you only have time to read one book to learn about real world economies, I recommend Jared Diamond's **Collapse**. [10] Studying the way real societies and economies fall apart is a great way to get a sense of how they worked.

GETTING MAGIC RIGHT

When we think of magic, synonyms like wonder, amazement, and supernatural come to mind. When we write about magic, particularly when we're creating fictional worlds in which magic plays a part, words like supply, demand and cost should be foremost in our minds. Economics seems about as far removed from magic as you can get, but it's the foundation of verisimilitude even when we're dealing with fantastic things.

One of the basic rules of economics is that given two equivalent items for sale, people, as rational economic actors, will always choose the one that is less expensive. When innovations come along that deliver the same or better experience for less, people abandon the old in favor of the new. With personal music collections, for example, CDs eclipsed vinyl records and then MP3 players became all the rage.

What does this have to do with magic?

What would happen to the world if people could conjure what they need and want with little thought or effort?

Commerce, specialization, and even initiative would

likely disappear. Much of what we strive for simply wouldn't be worth the bother. Most people, for example, no longer exert themselves to memorize multiplication tables now that calculators are ubiquitous. Most importantly, at least for writers, in a world where the price of anything you want is the wave of a wand, conflict goes away. In economic terms, without want (demand, and its implied willingness to pay a price) there is no market.

So what can you do if you have magic in your story? Are there any precedents that will give some degree of verisimilitude?

Arthur C. Clarke famously said, "Any sufficiently advanced technology is indistinguishable from magic." The smart phones many of us tote, for example, would give most lamp-based genies a run for their money (assuming adequate cell coverage during Arabian nights). So the best way to increase the verisimilitude of your magic system is to let your experience with advanced technology be your guide.

Holly Black suggested you ask yourself six questions about your magic system:

- Who has it?
- What does it do?
- How do you make it happen?
- How is the user affected?
- How is the world affected?
- How are magic users grouped & perceived?

In a similar vein, Brandon Sanderson (who has more experience with systematic magic than most of the rest of us) said, "Magic systems can fall anywhere in the spectrum from wonder-based to rule-based, but to be credible, there must be constraints and consequences."

That observation leads directly to Sanderson's First Law:

> "Your ability to solve problems in your book with magic is directly proportional to how well your reader understands the system of magic."

Sanderson suggests developing magic as you would the setting:

- Focus on an ability that isn't overused or give it a unique twist.

- Add an interesting cost to use that ability.

- Find good visuals that provide an interesting way to describe the magic as it is used.

- Include limitations on how the magic can be used—these are usually more interesting than the power itself.

As with just about everything else we've covered under the rubric of verisimilitude, rhyme and reason resonate more strongly than coincidence.

GETTING SCIENCE RIGHT

I attended a panel on, "Archeology in Science Fiction," at a writing convention. The presenters were credentialed archeologists and they gamely fielded questions from the audience about the scientific plausibility of various plot points.

As someone who also trained in the dusty science, it was fascinating to listen to the questions. The audience understood that contemporary archeology looks nothing like an Indiana Jones adventure. Nevertheless, the issues they raised betrayed a simplistic hope for drama and excitement.

Real science is less exciting than you think and more thrilling than you can imagine. Every wet lab I've been involved with has had to mix flasks of colored water for the photographers because real chemistry and biology usually happen in clear or slightly yellow liquids that make for dull pictures. But when you understand what's actually happening in the reaction vessel, it blows your mind in a way pictures never could.

One of the questions to the panelists was, "What's the coolest thing you've ever found on a dig?"

The coolest thing I found on a dig was a tiny pearl button, perhaps a quarter inch in diameter.

I trust you're suitably disappointed: how could a little button compare with the Staff of Ra or a pile of treasure?

Because of the context.

We were excavating a federal army outpost in southern New Mexico that was occupied for about ten years before the civil war. The button, which came from a dress—perhaps one that belonged to an officer's wife—spoke volumes about army logistics in frontier territories during the time following the Mexican-American war when the dominant trade routes in the region shifted from Mexico in the south to the U.S. in the east: specifically, that the post was civilized enough for women of status to live there.

What you need to know about science is that most of the time it's like a mystery where once you fully understand the context, one key piece of evidence can unlock the puzzle. It's rarely about drama because science is fundamentally about being as certain as possible that you know what you think you know. Drama, in contrast, flourishes in uncertainty.

To give the science in your fiction a degree of verisimilitude, approach it like a mystery, not a thriller.

* * *

The thread running through all the examples in this chapter is that verisimilitude depends upon plausibility. Plausibility can be implied, by getting the details right in one area and glossing over others, or explicit, through skillfully woven back story or explanations.

The one thing you must never do is under estimate your readers. Not only will they pick up every tiny inconsistency, they'll find implications you haven't imagined. Taking care to develop the verisimilitude of your story is simply a matter of respecting your readers by anticipating the questions they might have and skillfully weaving answers into your narrative.

CHAPTER 18.

PREPARATION AND WRITING INTENTIONALLY

Confidence is a funny word. Although we associate it with personalities and emotional states that range from quiet fortitude to bravado, its Latin roots mean, "with faith." In its original sense, the word means someone in whom we can put our faith and trust.

As readers, the single most important factor in our willingness to suspend our disbelief is the degree to which we trust the author, believe he or she has the story firmly under control, and have faith it will take us somewhere wonderful and worthwhile.

A confident author is like the nautical pilot, hand firmly on the tiller, who knows how to guide a ship safely through the reefs and into port. Nothing that happens in the story is accidental. And everything the author brings to our attention contributes to the ultimate aim of a satisfying story.

So what do you need to do to be a confident author?

It's not about bravado, but about control—and not the control of a commander shouting orders, but the control of the expert dancer or musician who makes what they do seem effortless. The confident author writes intentionally but with such craft that the reader, caught by the web of verisimilitude, is swept into the story and forgets it has an author.

DO YOU HAVE TO PREPARE BEFORE YOU WRITE?

Nathan Bransford said there are six things you should know before you start your novel: [11]

- Plot arc
- Obstacles
- Protagonist
- Setting
- Style and voice
- Climax

Many people who share writing advice divide the universe of writers into two camps: outliners and discovery writers (or, "plotters," and, "pantsers," if you like alliteration). A great deal of ink has been spilled over how each kind of writer works best (and what they should be excused from doing). Regardless of the camp into which you've been herded, there's one fundamental thing required of everyone who wants to write: You need to know enough so that you can write with confidence.

So, what does that mean for Nathan's list?

Even if you're a pure discovery writer, you must have some notion of where the story takes place (setting), who the protagonist is, what obstacles they face, where the story is going (climax), how you're going to get there (plot arc), and how you'll tell the story (style and voice). Otherwise you'll have the literary equivalent of a slow river: your text will meander but won't go anywhere—you'll write, but not intentionally.

And if you're an outliner, the list serves as a reminder you don't need to know every last detail: once you've worked out the six basic elements it's time to put pen to paper. If you hone your intent to a fine point but never get around to writing, you will have failed at the writing part of writing intentionally.

DISCOVER GARDENING

If you're a discovery writer, how do you write intentionally if you can't figure out your intentions until you've written the story and can look back over the ground you've covered to see the path that ties it all together?

Before you write a novel, you should have some idea of what your story is about and where it is going. There are certainly writers who start with an intriguing character or an interesting setting and develop a story around that nucleus. But if you don't have at least an inkling of where the story is headed, you run the risk that it won't go anywhere.

If you think of your writing as gardening instead of discovery, you can get past the fallacy that you don't have to plan ahead but can simply jump in and start writing. Gardeners don't throw seed out and wait to see what comes up. Based on their understanding of varieties and growing conditions, they plan which things to plant in different parts of the garden. Similarly, there's a fair amount of forethought that goes into deciding what kind of garden you want to grow. Is it a flower garden that will offer a changing canvas of shapes and colors as the season progresses? Or is the produce you'll harvest the main purpose of the garden?

Of course the gardener doesn't know whether a given seed will sprout and grow as intended. So they plant more than one. And they cultivate the garden, weeding, watering, and fertilizing, to make the desired outcome more likely.

Gardeners discover new things every day. Without preparation and cultivation, they're more likely to discover slugs and fungus instead of flowers and fruit. So too with your writing: if you take a little time to plan your story garden and prepare the soil of your imagination, you'll find your ability to write intentionally grows—like your garden.

ARCHITECTURE OVER OUTLINES

Someone who plans out every detail in advance is the poster child of intentional writing, right?

Not necessarily. There's such a thing as too much preparation.

I once interviewed with a company for a software development position, turned down the job, and then wound up working for them a year later. During the first visit, they showed me the design for the software package they planned to build. A year later, when I set to work actually implementing the software, I found stacks of paper with increasingly detailed designs, culminating in the pièce de résistance: printed flowcharts filled with code. Had they skipped the flow charts and put the code in source files, they likely would have had running software.

Writers, particularly those who work in the fantastic and need to create worlds with consistent history, economies, religions, languages, and magic systems are particularly prone to a malady that Brandon Sanderson calls, "world-building disease." It doesn't help that the mythology about the mythology of **The Lord of the Rings** makes much of the fact that J.R.R. Tolkien spent twenty years building his world before he wrote the novels.

Computer scientist Terry Winograd's answer to the tendency to over-specify software projects is a new vocation he calls, "software architect." Like real architects, they must be able to work across a range of concerns, going from a meeting with the structural engineer that's all about bearing loads to a meeting with a client who wants a house that says, "Soaring! ... In mauve!"

An architect is more flexible that you might assume.

The writer as architect needs to avoid the trap of forever planning and never writing. Your goal is not to fully specify the story. Instead it comes back to writing with confidence. The challenge for the writer as architect is to have faith that your preparations have been sufficient and that they provide a framework in which you can solve the story problems that will inevitably appear as you proceed.

And then write.

Don't fall into the trap of typing code into flow charts when you should be building running software.

THE RIGHT TOOL FOR THE JOB

We talk about the two great camps of writers, but there

are some who take different approaches for different projects. I want to indulge in a bit of heresy and suggest that there are different stories and contexts where one approach is more adaptive than the other. Specifically, fantastic stories require outlines and realistic stories need to be discovered.

With fantastic stories, which include things like murder mysteries and thrillers that take place in the real world, consistency is paramount if you want readers to suspend their disbelief.

With realistic stories, the world of our everyday experience is so full of elements with varying significance that you have to explore to discover which ones belong in the story.

Put another way, the two modes are not mutually exclusive. Rather, it is more useful to understand architecture and gardening as approaches to writing. Like the artist who may be more comfortable with one medium than another but uses the one that is most appropriate for the work, you may prefer one mode but you should be adept at each.

For my part, I like to outline at the chapter level, where I make note of key scenes and plot points, in order to be clear about what the chapter needs to accomplish, and then discover the details of what happens as I write each scene.

Fear about freedom is the real point of contention between the camps of outline and discovery writers. Plotters take comfort in their outlines because they're afraid of dead ends. Seat-of-the-Pantsers take comfort in chaotic creativity because they're afraid of constraints.

Writing, however, is an organic process: the book grows closer to its final form with each successive draft.

The decisions you make in one draft give you the framework to refine the details in the next. In the end, whether you prepare and outline or simply dive in and start writing, you'll wind up doing the same amount of work to craft a story worthy of other people's time and attention.

RESEARCH TECHNIQUES

How can you write about a real place you've never visited but which others know well? One common method is to draft the story you want to write and then enlist people who know the subject or setting to check your research and correct your errors.

If you can't visit in person, another obvious answer is to roll up your sleeves and do the research. Writers, however, have a particular challenge when it comes to travel and research: they generally can't afford to do it.

In an absolute sense, writing is illusion. So the critical question is how can you do just enough research to create a compelling illusion?

The biggest pitfall for a writer is to go with common wisdom or accept something at face value. Of course, we know not to do that with our characters and our plots: we avoid stereotypes and tired old plot devices by digging deeper into the character or story. But we forget that we need to dig deeper in our research.

If you go with common wisdom, or take things at face value, you will always make the kind of glaring mistakes that cause people who know more about the subject to dismiss your book, disgusted that you couldn't be bothered to take a few minutes to get the basic details right.

For example, we *know* that history is a story of progress

because we now have cities and luxuries on a scale that our ancestors couldn't imagine—never mind the fact that some people in the ancient world enjoyed many of the conveniences we assume are the unique province of our modern world.

Likewise, we *know* that medieval warriors bludgeoned each other with heavy, clumsy swords—never mind the fact that when someone actually studied real medieval combat swords they found common wisdom was wrong: fighting swords, unlike the oversized decorative and ceremonial ones that fill museums, were lighter, and, with the right fighting techniques, as agile and deadly as modern swords. [12]

When you want to write about something with which you are unfamiliar, begin with this guiding principle: people generally don't do things that don't make sense, and they almost never do things contrary to their own interests. Simply asking whose interests are being served often helps you zero in on the most important facets of the subject, whether it's a place, a person, or a process.

Remember, your goal is not to become a world-class expert on the subject, but to know enough to convince the experts you've done your homework by avoiding the obvious errors.

Here are two touchstones to help you know when you've done enough research:

- Your research isn't done until you've discovered something surprising about the topic.

- Your research isn't done until you can explain how the conventional wisdom is both right and wrong.

HOW MUCH DO YOU HAVE TO PREPARE?

Here's another of life's catch-22s: the best way to be part of a conversation is to have something new to say, but to be sure what you have to say is new you need to know the history of the conversation—which often means filling your head so full of what everyone else is saying you don't have anything to add. It's difficult to do something new and meaningful if you're ignorant of the conversation. On the other hand, there's so much to read that you could spend your life trying to get through it all and still be behind.

What's a busy writer to do?

The trick, of course, is to strike a balance: your job isn't to become an expert on the literature but to be familiar with what your readers would consider the main works.

There's a nice analogy with travel: you're not trying to become a tour guide, but you should know the area well enough that you can get around without having to ask for directions.

* * *

We periodically hear about hackers breaking into computer systems. The way the story is usually told gives us the impression hackers are cyber-witches with crypto-incantations beyond the ken of mortal men. It is true that there are some very clever people trying to find ways to gain unauthorized access to computer systems, but some of the high-profile cyber-attacks have been the result not of technical wizardry but a far more ancient art: social hacking.

It's no accident that one of the synonyms for con artist is, "confidence man." You can get far in pursuits both legal and not if you simply press forward confidently, acting as though you have every right to be there. But a successful social hack requires much more than moxie: you've got to be prepared to both look and act the part, taking particular care to not give anyone any reason to suspect you're not what you seem to be. It doesn't matter how confident you sound as you breeze past the security guards and tell them you're late for a board meeting, they'll throw you out if you're wearing a clown suit.

As a closing metaphor, social hacking is sure to win the ire of the upright citizens' brigade. Nevertheless, it is the essence of what you're up to when you create fiction. There are strong parallels between the successful techniques in both lines of endeavor. Perhaps the most significant difference is that the best writing flows from a profound respect for your readers.

All the techniques for improving the verisimilitude of your stories come back to respect. Beginning with the subject, your aim must be to engage your readers. The way in which you tell your story, from the scenes you show to your wordsmithing, must always reinforce, never dispel the illusion. Attention to detail so that conflicts ring true and the numbers add up shows your readers how much you care. And doing the preparation so that you can get things right is how you honor the people who take the time to read the book.

In the end, verisimilitude is a product of your ability to show your readers the rhyme and reason of your story by writing intentionally.

CHAPTER 19.

STORY DEVELOPMENT TOOLS

We all know people who intend to write but never produce anything. At the other extreme we find people who dash off reams of scenes and dialog but never pull it all together into a coherent whole. No matter how much you believe creativity is a matter of inspiration from notoriously fickle muses, it is a pragmatic fact that you can't complete a large-scale project without some organizing principles.

When I begin a project, I spend a lot of time writing but none of it advances my word count because I'm writing notes and essays to myself as I organize my thoughts. Here are two of the tools I've found essential when I'm developing a story.

STORY MAPS

Story Maps are not about what happens, but why. For those of you discovery writers whose hackles rise when you hear anything that sounds like a preplanned constraint, story maps are not plot outlines. They're maps of the motivational course of your characters through emotional time and space.

An intricately plotted story degenerates into a roller coaster ride without the trajectory of motivations that bring characters into conflict at certain times and places. A character driven story can easily veer off into the weeds if the characters aren't constrained by their motivational trajectory and can do whatever they want. Harry Potter, for example, wouldn't be Harry Potter if at some point he'd gotten fed up with the whole Voldemort business and settled in for some quality video gaming with Dudley.

J. Michael Straczynski argues, in **Bablyon 5**, that the two fundamental character questions are, "Who are you?" and, "What do you want?" A story map simply tracks how a character's answers to those questions change over time.

The form of a story map is far less important than its function. You can use the dreaded outline, draw it as a graph, write it out as part of your bible, or etch it on the moon with a giant laser (well, maybe not that last one).

STORY BIBLES

One of the most important enablers if you wish to write intentionally is a system to help you keep track of story details. Having someone notice that the hero's hair color changes halfway through the book (without an intervening trip to a stylist) is the literary equivalent of smiling with spinach on your teeth.

The best answer is to turn to a bible—a story bible, not **The Bible**.

When writers talk about story bibles, they mean a place to collect all the information that pertains to the story. The notion comes from episodic television where the producers had a document describing the situation and all the characters. They would give it to the writers brought on to pen different episodes so that the scripts they produced had a degree of consistency (e.g., you wouldn't want a character who is normally shy and retiring leap out to save the day in one episode and then go back to hiding under the table in the next).

When software architects design commercial data systems, they are careful to create a single source of truth. A story bible is really nothing more or less complicated than this. It can be physical, like a folder or a binder (bound books are probably not suitable because you'll want to add, remove, and arrange your material), or virtual (anything from a text file to a database, depending on your ambition). All that matters is that it's the one place where you can keep everything related to your story.

Don't let the word *bible* frighten you with visions of the formalities with which you must comply. You may, for example, come across suggestions that you subdivide your bible into sections on characters, settings, backstory, and so on. Those are reasonable ways to organize your material. You could also organize your story bible like an encyclopedia, with entries for each significant entity in your story. All that matters is that you have a way to organize your material so that:

1. You can easily find it again
2. You know where to add new material.

Remember, this is your resource. Don't worry about

how others have created and maintained story bibles. Find something that works for you.

Don't let the bible become something that takes so much time to maintain that you have no time left to write the story.

And above all, promise yourself that your story bible will forever be a private document—the information equivalent of what you look like when you get out of bed in the morning—so you're never tempted to try to make it presentable.

PART III.

CHARACTER AND ARCHETYPE

CHAPTER 20.

STRENGTH OF CHARACTER

I must confess: I like fantastic stories better than contemporary ones. Given that stories of the fantastic are usually not at the top of the list for careful character studies, it is, perhaps, not the most auspicious way to start a guide to character and archetypes. But trying to figure out why I prefer fantasy is what led to the study you now hold.

At first I feared I was simply too judgmental of characters in familiar situations. It's easy to question the choices characters in a contemporary story make when you can think of alternate courses of action. In a fantasy, where the rules are different, it's harder to second guess the characters. The issue, however, is deeper than characters doing things with which you don't agree: a story falls apart if a reader can think of other, simpler ways to solve the story problem. For example, there are a great many romances in which the couple is kept apart at some point by a misunderstanding that could be resolved with a five-minute conversation.

Regardless of the setting, whether fantastic or realistic,

in order for your characters to ring true, readers must believe their actions are natural and inevitable. Readers fold every bit of character information you give them into a mental model. Behavior which reinforces the model feels natural. Behavior which extends the model feels inevitable. Where your readers are familiar enough with the context to imagine alternatives, you've got to take greater care to establish why your characters wouldn't or couldn't behave differently.

Another difference I noted between fantastic and realistic stories is the relative degree of activity and passivity. In one well-reviewed and highly recommended contemporary novel, much of the interaction takes place while the characters are hanging out. Fantastic stories tend to have a lot less hanging out because the characters are trying to do something—to get someplace, find something, or unravel a mystery. Contemporary stories are often about making one's way in society by finding friends and fitting in. Fantasy is almost never about fitting in, it's about being extraordinary.

You might rightly point out that my view of narrative activity and passivity is subjective and argue that characters trying to understand themselves and their place in a complex world are every bit as active as heroes battling villains. I am guilty as charged: I prefer stories which entertain the possibility that we might be wonderful over those whose fundamental world view is that life is something to be endured and which, at best, offer the hope that we might cope.

But again, there's something important here that goes beyond my entertainment preferences. Story is about change over time. In character terms that means story is about people who do interesting things—who engage life and the world around them—and who reveal their character through their actions.

STRONG CHARACTERS

If we're supposed to cheer for the hero and hiss at the villain, why is the bad-guy often the strongest character in the story?

Good antagonists, of course, believe they are the hero of their own story. On the strength of that conviction, they act. Their actions, in turn, harm or threaten the hero, which sets the story in motion. The protagonist usually spends the first half of the story reacting because the antagonist has the initiative. We learn about each character through the things they do, but we learn more from actions than reactions—which is important insofar as the antagonist is concerned because we need to understand his or her character well enough to side with the protagonist.

So what makes a strong character?

First, character is what makes a person interesting. Someone who has no opinions, interests, or aspirations—who exists in perfect compliance—isn't interesting. An interesting character has their own view and agenda, and they make their own decisions.

Second, character is the sum of a person's actions over time. We often fall into the error of reducing character to the initial description and first impressions. While a person's appearance may provide some evidence of their character, we come away from a single meeting with nothing more than a caricature of them. It's only after we've observed their behavior in different times and places that we understand them well enough to predict how they'll react in a new situation.

It's easy to get confused when we talk about strong characters because when we describe someone in real life as a, "strong character," we often mean that they're overbearing or obnoxious. Strong characters in narrative are simply interesting people whose actions give us insight into who they are.

STRONG FEMALE CHARACTERS

Strength, particularly physical strength, is generally a male attribute. What do we mean by *strong* when we're talking about female characters?

For reasons ranging from biology to culture, the ways in which men and women can or are expected to show strength differ. That said, the things that make a strong female character are the same things that make a strong male character: a sense of purpose and the will to act.

Viewed in this light, strength of character and femininity are perfectly compatible. Most women may not be able to go toe-to-toe with the men in a barroom brawl, but they often exceed the males in the quiet, daily kind of strength. Similarly, women often show strength by drawing together a society who can collectively solve a problem instead of attacking it head-on. And unlike men who equate vulnerability with weakness, women are often strongest when they acknowledge their vulnerabilities.

Persistence in the face of opposition is a common sign of strength of character. A person who states a position and then changes his or her mind when someone counters with a contrary opinion is a weak character. A strong character has courage, in the particular sense that they don't give up easily—not because they're pig-headed, but because they know what they believe and why they believe it.

Strength of character is never measured on an absolute scale. It's only meaningful in light of a character's weaknesses. That a strong, healthy man who is versed in combat steps up to fight reveals less about his character than a physically weaker woman reveals about hers when she does something similar.

The best strategy is to approach each character, regardless of gender, as an individual with their own mix of strengths and weaknesses.

CHOICES REVEAL CHARACTER

Fiction requires one more thing of strong characters: they must be problem solvers. It may sound like the pinnacle of courage when the black knight stands on the bridge and declares, "None shall pass!" but you don't have a story if no one wants to pass and he's simply standing guard. Strong characters try things, fail, learn from their experience, and try again. And in doing so, they show us what they're made of.

The best way to show strength in narrative is to give the character two choices. If a character has consistently chosen safety over conflict during the course of a story, and if at the end they are offered a safe and honorable way out, the fact that they stay and fight says a great deal more than if they are simply cornered and have no choice.

* * *

There is, of course, much more to creating strong characters. In the next chapter, we look at the techniques of natural characterization. Chapter three focuses on character dynamics: the hierarchy of needs that motivate characters and the universal human pattern of reactions. Beyond simply being active and interesting, the most compelling characters transform˙ themselves over the course of a story. Through their experience we come to a better understanding of our own transformations. The majority of this book is dedicated to a study of the two archetypical patterns of transformation: the hero's journey in chapter four and the virgin's promise in chapter five. We turn to romance in chapter six, and conclude, in chapter seven, with an approach to unifying character and plot.

But if you get nothing more from this book than the understanding that strong characters have a sense of who they are, what they want, and what they're willing to do—that, above all, are active—you'll improve your writing by an order of magnitude.

CHAPTER 21.

NATURAL CHARACTERIZATION

Character is, "The sum of qualities which distinguish one person or thing from another." (Webster 1886) It is something, as social animals, to which we are exquisitely attuned. While no book, regardless of its length, can capture the full complexity of a living, breathing person, with the tools of natural characterization you can give your readers not caricatures but characters who feel real.

FIXING UNLIKABLE CHARACTERS

Once, whilst possessed by a flippant mood, my answer to someone wondering how to fix her unlikable characters was, "Add cute animals: Darth Vader + kitten = problem solved, right?"

Likability, of course, has more dimensions than good or bad. It's one thing to give the villain some justification because something in his past turned him to evil. But what do you do, for example, about contemporary characters that are unlikable because they're annoying, or tiresome?

A simplistic answer is to change the character so they're

no longer annoying or tiresome. That answer, though, masks a deeper question that you, the author, need to ask explicitly (because your readers will ask it implicitly) about every one of your character: why would I want to spend time with this person?

Does that mean your characters have to be nice in order to be likable?

Some novelists complain, "Life isn't always nice. Some people are unlikable. How can we show you what life is really like if we have to do, 'nice?'"

If your goal is to show life as it really is shouldn't you put as much energy into painting incisive and nuanced portraits of people who lead utterly unremarkable lives—who put the bore into boring?

"Not if you want anyone to read it," you might say. "People already know life can be boring."

And that's the point: people already know.

Readers expect to get something in return for the time they put into a book. When readers say a character is unlikable, they're really saying they find it difficult to see why it's worth investing their time in the character.

So what is it we're asking for when we say we want likable characters?

We're asking for some reason to like spending time with them.

Regardless of how morally reprehensible they are, we like characters that are interesting—that give us some insight or teach us something. Readers are willing to go to dark places to expand their horizons if they can follow characters with whom they can identify (i.e., likable) through a story that shows them something they didn't already know.

CHARACTER FLAWS

Relatability, which lies between empathy and familiarity, is closely tied to likability. A relatable character is one you understand at some level and into whose situation you can project yourself.

In an effort to make your characters more likable, you may be tempted to pour all your aspirations into them, making them good where you wish you were better. But a character that is too good is as unlikable as one that is reprehensible.

Perfect characters aren't very interesting. Superman without Kryptonite and his ethics is simply a demigod, unconstrained by the limitations of mere mortals. It's much more interesting—and more consistent with our experience of the people around us—to read about someone with an identifiable mix of strengths and weaknesses. While we may not understand a character's expertise or ability, we can all relate to feelings of inadequacy.

But there's an important difference between characters with flaws and characters that are stupid. Characters with flaws believe they are good, moral people who are trying to do the best they know how. Characters that are stupid know what they are doing is wrong or self-destructive but do it any way.

"Wait," you may say, as you rise up in righteous wrath, "there are really people like that in the world and I have a duty to tell it like it is."

To be clear, I'm not arguing for stories that are all sunshine and flowers. Indeed, there's a grand tradition of cautionary tales whose purpose is to warn by showing us the full extent of the tragedy. I'm arguing for strong characters.

A character headed for tragedy along a trajectory that makes sense (at least from their perspective) is far more interesting, and far stronger, than a character that knowingly fails because they haven't the energy or strength of will to get off the couch and do something.

APPROPRIATE SELF-CONSCIOUSNESS

In Orson Scott Card's book **Characters and Viewpoint**, he says the following about cleverness:

> "Notice that I don't use the word intelligence. That's because in our society with its egalitarian ideals, any obvious display of intelligence or erudition suggests elitism, snobbery, arrogance."
>
> "Yet we love a character who is clever enough to think of solutions to knotty problems. Does this seem contradictory? It is contradictory."[1]

This is something that hits close to home for me. It took me a while to learn that my attempts to be precise and thorough were often off-putting in exactly the way Card describes.

I enjoy stories about smart people tested to their limits much more than stories about not-so-smart people whose problems are largely self-imposed and could be avoided with a bit of sense. For example, the movie **Jurassic Park** would have been a far better cautionary tale without the sabotage subplot. Instead of showing that life can't be controlled by even the best and brightest among us, it suggests an amusement park full of resurrected dinosaurs could have worked if some people hadn't been greedy.

So what can you do if you want characters that are both bright and likable?

Card's solution is:

> "You have to walk a fine line, making [your character] very clever without ever letting [them] be clever enough to notice how clever [they] are."

In other words, likable characters must not be overly self-conscious. Like a child who is cute until they realize they're cute, characters who flaunt their charisma and abilities alienate readers. If Harry Potter had swaggered around Hogwarts bragging to all the impressionable young witches that he was the chosen one, we would have cheered when Voldemort took him out. Instead, like all heroes, his self-deprecation—born of a natural and relatable fear that he wouldn't be up to the task—was one of the fundamental aspects of his character that endeared him to readers the world over.

SEAMLESS CHARACTERIZATION

Similarly, the ways in which we show our characters to our readers should not be overly self-conscious. Telling readers a character is a certain way actually makes that character less likable than allowing the reader to form their own picture and make their own judgment. It's not enough that you make sure your clever character never notices how clever they are, you must take care not to be noticeably clever in the way you reveal your clever character.

The flow of character information should be barely distinguishable from all the other information in the story. One way to achieve a seamless blend is to find ways to convey more than one kind of information in your narrative. For example, metaphors convey far more information than ordinary phrases or sentences because of the associations that arise from the comparison. If metaphors flow from the character, particularly in internal monologue, the objects they choose for comparison tell us about the character as well as what they may be thinking or feeling. Each character has a unique mix of competence and experience to draw upon when they need a metaphor.

You should, however, resist the temptation to rely too heavily on idiosyncratic, character-based metaphors, particularly in a fantasy where the reader doesn't know the character's referential context. (Does, "He was as happy as a skurlump on a fringbol," mean anything to you?) That said, not only are a few well-chosen character-based metaphors a key part of the voice of the narrative, character-based metaphors are also a good way to avoid anachronisms when you're writing about another time or place.

BACKSTORY IS STORY

The same technique of using character to color narrative applies to every story element in which character can play an active role.

One of the common missed opportunities for unobtrusive characterization is backstory. Writers tend to think of backstory as everything the reader should know about what happened before the beginning of the narrative in order to truly appreciate the story. Often the burden of backstory is so great authors give in to the sin of the info dump—an expository section that breaks up the narrative. While disrupting the pacing of the story is serious enough, info dumping squanders your golden opportunity to use backstory to convey information about your characters.

When you're getting acquainted with someone (and they with you), do you give them a resume that lists your accomplishments? No, once we get past the small talk, we trade stories.

We understand ourselves largely in terms of the stories we tell about ourselves. And we tell different stories to different people and at different times.

Think about yourself and your characters as you consider the following questions:

- What stories do you tell about yourself when you meet people?

- How do you tell those stories?

- What stories do you choose not to tell when you meet people?

- Are there situations in which you would tell the stories you usually avoid?

- What stories do you tell only to yourself?

Action reveals character. The stories your characters choose to tell, and the way in which they tell them, speaks volumes. If you haven't nailed the voice, ask your character to introduce themselves to you.

More generally, don't ask how your character would react, ask how they did react.

* * *

Natural characterization is an art that you will struggle to perfect as long as you write. But you can dramatically improve your characters if you know why readers will want to spend time with them, understand that the most interesting characters have a mix of strengths and weaknesses, and aren't overly self-conscious. And you can dramatically improve your characterization by seamlessly blending it into the story and coloring every aspect of the narrative so that it also reveals something about a character.

CHAPTER 22.

CHARACTER DYNAMICS

People are endlessly fascinating: we want to know why they do what they do. Because of that life-long study, when a reader complains your characters aren't realistic they're actually saying that something about your characters doesn't accord with their expectations about how people behave.

There are two fundamental dynamics that drive how we act and how we react. We are motivated to act by our needs, real or perceived, and we react according to a pattern you may know as the grief cycle. These are, of course, generalizations. But they're common enough that if your characters are going to behave differently, and you don't want readers throwing your book across the room, you must take care to show why your character's behavior makes sense in this particular situation.

CHARACTERS, EXPECTATIONS, AND THE MASLOW HIERARCHY

Abraham Maslow proposed a hierarchy of needs in his 1943 paper, *A Theory of Human Motivation*. [2] Maslow's hierarchy is often presented as a pyramid to emphasize the way in which each tier of needs depends upon the one beneath. That is, people generally don't worry about needs at a higher level until they've satisfied their needs at a lower level.

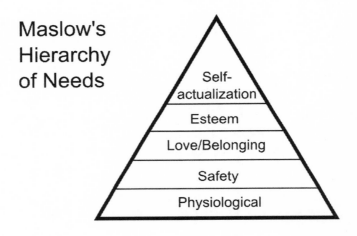

Maslow's Hierarchy of Needs

- Self-actualization
- Esteem
- Love/Belonging
- Safety
- Physiological

Starting at bottom, or most basic level, Maslow suggested that our needs are:

1. **Physiological**: breathing, food, water, sex, sleep, homeostasis, excretion
2. **Safety**: security of body, employment, resources, morality, the family, health, property
3. **Love/Belonging**: friendship, family, sexual intimacy
4. **Esteem**: self-esteem, confidence, achievement, respect of others, respect by others
5. **Self-actualization**: morality, creativity, spontaneity,

problem solving, lack of prejudice, acceptance of facts

Characters should generally work their way up the hierarchy. This means, for example, that your readers will cry foul if your characters stop in the midst of deadly peril to worry about their self-esteem or have a romantic liaison during a gun-battle.

But it reveals a great deal about a character if they violate a lower-level need in favor of a higher level need. For example, someone may place themselves in danger, violating their need for safety, if by doing so they can save a loved one, satisfying their need for love and belonging.

In order to get away with violating readers' common sense about the hierarchy of needs, you must establish the character's overriding need before they act against expectations.

The other lesson from Maslow's hierarchy is that characters are more realistic and more compelling if their behavior is driven by needs at more than one level in the hierarchy.

THE CONSERVATION OF PERSONALITY

While you're taking care to be consistent with the hierarchy of needs, you also need to be consistent with the conservation of personality: characters won't act against personality, and personality doesn't change.

If you have a character who is shy and retiring, they won't grab the mike at the karaoke bar just because the plot calls for a diversion. Pushing something over without anyone noticing would be more consistent with their personality.

There are volumes about the psychology of personality and you could easily spend a lifetime studying such things. The key for busy writers who want strong characters is consistency. This doesn't mean your characters can never change—in fact they must—but the nature of the change must be consistent with their personality. In the same way that you say, "Of course I should've seen it coming," when the detective reveals whodunit in a mystery, character change, particularly actions or reactions that seem inconsistent with personality, must be foreshadowed and shown to be consistent at a deeper level.

THE ARC OF CHARACTER REACTIONS

According to conventional psychology, the process of grieving involves five stages: denial, anger, bargaining, depression, and acceptance. But that progression of reactions isn't limited to grief. Most of our reactions involve some or all of these stages, though often not felt as keenly.

More formally, the stages of denial, anger, bargaining, depression, and acceptance summarize the hierarchy of reaction strategies.

Consider a primitive encounter in which a stranger approaches:

1. **Denial**: the simplest reaction strategy is to ignore the newcomer. If they lose interest and leave, you've dealt with them at no cost to yourself.
2. **Anger**: if the stranger won't go away, a brief show of aggression might drive them off. If they run away, you've dealt with them at only a small cost.

3. **Bargaining**: if the stranger isn't spooked, you might try bribing them to leave. This is more costly, but it still resolves the situation quickly.
4. **Depression**: the stranger still won't go away and now you despair of finding a solution.
5. **Acceptance**: you realize the stranger isn't going away and you find a way to cope with that fact.

The pattern arises from our instinctive desire to resolve situations at the lowest possible cost. Loss, and its attendant grief, takes a character through all five stages because there is no solution that will restore the lost object. But other kinds of interactions can end at an earlier stage. For example, take the stereotypical presentation of a bad report card:

Child: Here, you have to sign this.
 Parent: What is it?
 Child: My report card?
 Parent: There must be some mistake. [Denial]
 Child: No, it's mine.
 Parent: You knucklehead! How could … [Anger]

If, at that point, the child mumbled about doing better, that could be the end of the episode. (Of course, the reality most of us experience, as both the child and the parent, almost certainly involves bargaining and probably a fair amount of depression.)

The key observation is that most character reactions should follow this sequence of responses, in this order, even if the encounter doesn't go through all five stages.

Watching the people around you, you may not be convinced that character dynamics can ever be mastered. The patterns of motivation and reaction presented in this chapter may not be enough to understand the people with whom you must deal, but they are the foundation upon which strong, believable characters are built.

CHAPTER 23.

THE HERO'S JOURNEY

In his book, **The Hero with a Thousand Faces**, Joseph Campbell [3] developed a theory of the monomyth, or hero's journey, [4] based on archetypes that recur in stories from around the world and across time. A full discussion of Campbell's contribution and all the subsequent work in the area by anthropologists, mythologist, psychologists, and their ilk is way beyond our scope, but authors and screenwriters have distilled the narrative essence of the hero's journey into a framework that maps the arc of a character's transformation.

Christopher Vogler's, **The Writer's Journey**, provides a practical condensation of the mythic structure of the hero's journey to twelve key phases. [5]

The Ordinary World: we meet the restless would-be hero and see the worthy community in which he lives.

The Call to Adventure: the hero learns that something is amiss—a growing peril threatens the hero's ordinary world.

Refusing the Call: whether because of obligations, lack of preparation, or some sense of the difficulties in store, the hero declines the call in favor of the safety of the ordinary world.

Meeting the Mentor: the hero is rescued from his fears, or from trouble caused by his naivety, by someone who has been down a similar road and survived.

Crossing the Threshold: the hero passes the point of no return and commits himself to the journey.

Tests, Allies, and Enemies: the hero explores the special world, learning who he can and cannot trust.

Approach to the In-most Cave: with the help of his new allies, the hero prepares to confront the peril.

The Ordeal: the hero discovers the true scope of the peril, often at the cost of some of his allies, and barely escapes with his life.

The Reward: but the hero doesn't come away from the ordeal empty-handed—though the cost was high, the hero retrieved an object or gained information that makes it possible to defeat the peril.

The Road Back: with full knowledge of the scope of the peril, and the fate that likely awaits him, the hero chooses the path that will lead to the final battle.

The Final Battle and Resurrection: drawing upon all his resources, particularly his heretofore unknown internal strength, the hero transcends certain death to defeat the peril.

Return with the Elixir: the hero returns to his community a new man, using the power he has gained through his journey to bring healing and peace.

The stories we tell often involve elements of the hero's journey. Each time we write a book we take a journey like the hero's: through the arduous process of writing, we become the protagonists of the story of how the book came to be. The parallels between the story we express and the experience of expressing that story are strong and significant to our personal development as writers as well as the development of our characters.

Using well-known examples from **Star Wars Episode IV** and **The Lord of the Rings**, we will examine each of these stages, not only as a way of structuring our stories and their character arcs, but also as aspects of our experience as writers.

THE ORDINARY WORLD

The hero's journey, which in essence is the transition, both physically and psychologically, from dependence to independence, begins in the *Ordinary World*.

As the bedrock of our common experience, it's easy to ignore, dismiss, or discount the ordinary world, both in our lives and our stories, because we're anxious to get to the interesting things that only happen when the hero undertakes the journey.

At the most basic level, the ordinary world provides the context for and counterpoint to the hero's journey. Memories of the ordinary, simple pleasure of the Shire, for example, sustain Frodo and Sam while suffering the rigors of their journey in **The Lord of the Rings**, and fear of what might happen to their home if they fail keeps them going.

The ordinary world is also the locus—perhaps threatened, or lost when the story begins—of safety and security. This is a critical element in the hero's journey because leaving the ordinary world means crossing from the known to the unknown, the tame to the wild, the safe to the unsafe, the light to the dark.

The hero's journey for writers begins in the ordinary world of readers, where we are dependent on others for the stories that delight us. Whether our love grows or cools as we find more to read, over time we notice our dependence and toy with the notion we might someday become authors too.

In the ordinary world of readers, we are largely ignorant of the publishing world and the often perverse ways in which it works. There are two practical consequences of this ignorance.

The first is that we enjoy the luxury of criticism. We can declare books good or bad with impunity on the strength of the fact that as readers our opinion is the only one that matters.

The second is that we grossly underestimate the effort required to produce a book. For example, there are plenty of people who look at picture books and think it would be trivial to knock out a few hundred simple words and send it off to the illustrator. Looking at a book, we have no idea how many agonizing revisions it took to get from the first draft to the finished product.

Even those of us who have finished a novel find ourselves starting again from the ordinary world when we undertake a new project: completing the last one brought us to a safe place which we have to leave if we want to write another book.

THE CALL TO ADVENTURE

The hero's journey begins when life in the *Ordinary World* is interrupted by a *Call to Adventure*. The call may be a direct or indirect threat to the village, news of wrongs to be set right and great deeds to be done, or simply the feeling that life is passing the hero by and greater opportunities are to be found elsewhere.

In terms of story structure, the call to adventure is the inciting incident, the event that starts the journey. It is the thing that makes it impossible, at least for the hero, to continue life in the ordinary world: either he steps up and undertakes the journey or he lives in terrible anticipation of what is coming or what could have been. When Frodo realizes he must take the ring from the Shire, when Luke stumbles upon Leia's message in R2D2, when Jim Hawkins learns he has a map to Treasure Island—each of these characters is at a point where, regardless of what they do next, nothing will be the same.

This is why the first critical skill for storytellers is identifying the inciting incident. Specifically, what out of the mix of setting, circumstance, and character makes it impossible for your protagonist to continue with their safe, comfortable life in the ordinary world?

Those of us who take up the pen experience a similar call to adventure. Perhaps it was the danger of a layoff, the wrong of one bad book too many thrown across the room, the restlessness of a dream too long deferred, the temptation of famous authors laughing all the way to the bank, or a really good idea that simply wouldn't leave you alone.

You may not be able to point to a dramatic (or even specific) event that set you on your way, but there was a point at which you stopped toying with the notion of writing and started writing. I know of several authors, for example, who banged out a chapter or a short story to prove to themselves or others that they couldn't do it—and wound up proving the opposite.

The notion that you could do it—not in the idle sense of declaring a book, "crap," and boasting you could do better, but the knowledge bubbling up from the deeper, behavior-changing well of motivation that you have enough talent, skill, and determination to produce a novel—changes everything: you can no longer be content simply reading other people's work.

Established writers have a similar experience, reaching a point where (for reasons from the practical—like having a contract for another book—to the personal—simply wanting to do better) they can no longer be content with the work they have done.

What is consistent, whether we're talking about your protagonist or your experience as a writer, is that the call to adventure is a heady thing because it is fraught with both peril and promise.

REFUSING THE CALL

The thrill of the possibilities offered by the *Call to Adventure* is inevitably followed by the terror of all that could go wrong and the temptation to *Refuse the Call*. This is the point at which the hero begins to realize that it's a matter of life and death—specifically, his.

Death may seem overly melodramatic. The structural key is that there is no heroism and, more importantly, no opportunity for growth if there are no risks. Which is not to say that the hero must understand the full scope of what he'll have to face: the hero simply realizes that the adventure could cost him more than he's ever had to pay. When Luke refuses Obi-wan's invitation to come to Alderaan and learn the ways of the force, he does so out of fear of his uncle, not legions of storm troopers and the Empire's ultimate weapon.

The other key structural point is that while both the hero and the coward initially refuse the *Call to Adventure*, the hero reconsiders and accepts. The acceptance may be reluctant, or even compelled—Luke had nothing to keep him on Tatooine and a very good reason to go with Obi-wan after the Imperials destroyed his home and killed his family—but unlike the coward, once the hero sets off he doesn't look back.

None of us believe writing a novel carries with it the risk of death (although there are enough dissidents and free-thinkers who have wound up on the receiving end of the full weight of the legal systems to which they were subject that we have to admit it's a possibility). But you do run a real risk of dying an emotional or social death should you fail.

What if you're wasting your time?

What if you're no good?

What if everyone finds out you're no good?

What if you don't like it but can't stop because you told everyone you were going to be a writer?

There's no end to the doubts and the fears because most of them are rational. Like the hero in the story, there are real, non-trivial things at stake for you personally as you face this undertaking.

These fears are natural.

They're also necessary.

The worth of the prize to be won is directly proportional to the risk of failure.

MEETING THE MENTOR

If the hero doesn't start with a mentor, his first steps on the journey only serve to get him into trouble, either by going the wrong way or antagonizing the people he meets.

The mentor or guide is critical to the hero's journey. First, as someone who has been down the road (or one like it) before, they are living proof it can be done and that the hero isn't crazy for trying. Second, the mentor helps the hero stop floundering and sets them on the proper path.

The mentor may rescue the hero from his initial mistakes, give him time and space to recover, help him prepare for the journey to come, and prod him when he's ready to go forward.

KEEPING THE HERO ALIVE

The hero needs a mentor because he lacks perspective, particularly when it comes to self-assessment. The hero sets off, after he decides not to *Refuse the Call*, overconfident, perhaps wildly optimistic. A setback may send him to the other emotional extreme.

Think about how crushing it was the first time someone rejected your first manuscript. It likely shook your entire sense of identity and self-worth as a writer.

Leaving the *Ordinary World* means leaving safety and comfort. The hero often realizes he is beyond accustomed help when he gets knocked down, either literally or figuratively. The mentor is generally the one who picks the hero up and provides a temporary refuge while he recovers and prepares.

PREPARING FOR THE TASK

Preparation and training are the most obvious ways a mentor helps the hero. Because of his or her knowledge and experience, the mentor guides the hero to focus on the skills and aspects of character that will matter most during the journey and its attendant trials.

For a writer, the preparation is largely a matter of craft and, if you're fortunate, art. Much of what you think of as, "the rules," is actually guidance to steer you away from rookie mistakes. At a higher level, it often takes a mentor to show you the art behind the craft, like how much narrative business—waking up and looking in the mirror and going down to breakfast and so on—you should skip because it interferes with the real story by obscuring the parts that matter.

NUDGING FORWARD

Mentors, because they are in a position to give the hero a more honest appraisal, provide perspective. They help the hero recognize and correct weaknesses. But the greatest gift they give the hero is telling him when he's ready to go.

MENTORS FOR WRITERS

The *Call to Adventure* is the moment when you get serious about your writing and actually put pen to paper. Even though writing is a solitary endeavor, you can't get very far down the path without some external validation. While it's gratifying if friends and family respond well to your early attempts, you generally don't make real progress until you *Meet the Mentor*.

In stories, it's far more effective if the mentor is a specific character. As a writer who lives in a complex, over-scheduled, information-rich world, you might find mentors in forums, blogs, books, conference, classes, critique groups, and writing friends, as well as among teachers and professionals. Whether your mentors are actual or virtual, their structural role in the journey is to give you perspective at a time when you have none.

CROSSING THE THRESHOLD

On January 10, 49 BC, Caesar led his legion across the river Rubicon and started the civil war that would end the Roman Republic. Once he moved his army across the provincial boundary—something the Senate had made illegal—there was no going back: he would either triumph or be destroyed.

To, "cross the Rubicon," is to go past the point of no return and commit to a course of action. While Caesar didn't complete a hero's journey to become Dictator of Rome, when he crossed the river he enacted the fifth phase of that journey: *Crossing the Threshold*.

The hero's journey doesn't truly get underway until the hero passes the point of no return. This is simply because prior to *Crossing the Threshold* there is little or no cost in turning back. Once past the threshold, turning back becomes extremely difficult, if not impossible.

In classic stories, this point is often a literal threshold where stepping across to the other side changes everything. This discontinuity makes the threshold magical—even sacred—though that quality may only be clear in retrospect.

When writing, particularly in the long form, there is a time where you commit to the story: your concept of the project changes from, "Can I do it?" to, "I can do it." Indeed, the commitment often takes the stronger form of, "Now I have to do it." Perhaps you told all your friends and family you were writing a book and can't face the shame of saying you gave up. Perhaps you've fallen in love with the story and need to know how it all ends. Perhaps it's simply the realization that the time and effort you've already spent on the project will be wasted if you don't finish. Whatever the reason, your journey into the unknown begins in earnest when abandoning the project is no longer an option.

Now you've left behind the safe realm where you know how things work and are striding into the wild lands where anything is possible.

Welcome to the undiscovered country of the writers.

TESTS, ALLIES, AND ENEMIES

In the sixth phase of the hero's journey, *Test, Allies, and Enemies*, the hero learns how to make his way in the *Special World*, overcoming challenges and learning who to trust and who to watch out for.

In **Star Wars**, for example, Luke finds allies in the cantina, tests his skills on the way to Alderaan, and meets his enemies on the Death Star. Of course, even that narrative is more complex because each of those sequences had its own series of tests and training to prepare Luke for the *Final Battle*. In terms of the hero's journey, the key is that Luke starts as a farm boy very much out of his element and ends, as they battle the Tie fighters before they can make good their escape from the Death Star, as a budding hero (who still needs to be reminded not to get cocky).

With the montage, films have a powerful idiom for conveying the fact that the characters have been occupied for some period of time without boring the audience by showing a sampling of the highlights or representative moments of those activities.

Unfortunately, life and narrative diverge because in

real journeys this phase is the part that takes most of the time. We have to live through all the moments that end up on the cutting room floor when the editor makes the montage.

That's not to say that the phase of tests, allies, and enemies is something tedious we must endure. It is, in fact, the substance of what we learn and how we transform ourselves on the journey.

As a writer, this is the time when you actually produce a draft. Your skills as a wordsmith and storyteller are tested, you find allies—whether figurative or literal—that help you write, and enemies that block your progress.

And most importantly, unlike your protagonists who only have to go through the narrative highlights, you need patience and faith to do all the hard work of passing the tests, developing your skills, finding allies, and identifying enemies required to produce a manuscript.

APPROACH TO THE IN-MOST CAVE

In the mythic form of the hero's journey, something critical—a talisman, a weapon, or simply a key bit of information—lies hidden and guarded in a cave. The hero and the allies he gathered in the sixth phase now understand enough about the *Special World* to attempt to enter the cave and obtain the critical element.

This phase is about preparation and a growing unity of purpose. At a high level, the first half of many stories is about what happens to the protagonists and the second half is about what the protagonists do. The *Approach to the In-most Cave* is the first substantive attempt to solve the story problem by confronting the antagonist directly. During the approach, whether literal or figurative, the hero and his allies plan the operation, inventory the dangers, and clarify the objective. They know they're not ready for the *Final Battle*, but this endeavor will strengthen them and/or weaken their enemy.

For writers, this phase corresponds to working with critique groups and beta readers to revise and polish the manuscript in preparation for submission.

Agents and editors, as much as they say they open every query hoping to find the next big thing, are structurally handicapped by the volume of material they receive and must, as a matter of survival, stop reading as soon as they find one too many problems. Getting past all the automatic reasons the people you query have to say, "No," is very much like infiltrating the villain's lair—not that agents and editors are villains but rather that the effort to stand out amid all the other queries is analogous to getting past the defenses. So you and your allies go through the drafts of the manuscript, synopsis, and query, sharpening and strengthening everything until you're ready to launch your submission.

And in that quite moment when you survey your work and realize you are prepared as you can be, there's a delicious mix of confidence, excitement, and a sprinkling of anxiety to savor as you nod and think this could actually work.

THE ORDEAL

Having gathered *Allies* and made preparations on the way to *The In-most Cave*, in the mythic cycle the hero and his party undergo an *Ordeal*. Some people also call this, *The Crisis*.

The key structural point is that, all his preparations notwithstanding, the crisis shows the hero that he didn't understand important elements or the full scope of the opposition. In the mythic cycle, this beat is the near-death or false death experience. The hero barely escapes with his life. Often the hero loses allies during the ordeal, which drives home the life and death stakes and, more importantly, gives the hero full knowledge of what he must face when he chooses to take *The Road Back* to the *Final Battle*.

While there are any number of things that can go wrong on your journey as a writer, the single biggest ordeal is rejection.

The first round of rejection is particularly challenging because you put so much effort into polishing the manuscript before submitting that it's hard to believe there's anyone who wouldn't like your story.

And largely because of that effort, the rejections unleash monsters of self-doubt: if all those industry pros don't like it, the story can't be as good as you thought—and, by extension, you can't be as good as you thought. So, why are you even trying?

This is the moment in the cycle when the hero is overshadowed by death.

This is the moment when many writers succumb, because no amount of hearing you should expect rejection prepares you for the reality of the pain that comes when something into which you've poured so much love, effort, and devotion is rejected.

Even if you know at a rational level that, given the number of competing manuscripts, your chances are slim, it doesn't lessen the sting of the rejection.

Even if you've been down the publishing road before, and have already suffered more than your fair share of rejections, the second, or fourth, or ninth time doesn't hurt any less (because you think you should know how to do it right by now).

So what do you do?

The hero in the journey pushes on, strengthened by the fact that he faced death and lived. And, painful though it was, he's learned or acquired something (though he may not fully understand it yet) that will help him in the *Final Battle*.

THE REWARD

While I believe there's a special ring of Hell reserved for public school coaches who say, "That which doesn't kill us makes us stronger," the hero's journey provides the kernel of truth to this old saw. Having faced the *The Crisis*, and lived to tell the tale, the hero now knows the real nature of the antagonist.

Knowledge and empowerment are the key outcomes of this phase. The hero now finally understands the scope of the threat and what's truly at stake. Often, the hero has also managed to acquire something that will prove critical in the *Final Battle*. For example, when Luke and Han blast their way out of the Death Star, they have the knowledge (in R2D2) and the means (Leia and her connection with the rebellion) to destroy the Empire's ultimate weapon.

That information provides both renewed determination and the insight or ability to defeat the antagonist. While the cost has been high, there is a clear sense that the hero gained something from *The Ordeal*. At this point the hero takes a moment to understand and celebrate *The Reward* for his efforts.

The writers who complete their own hero's journey emerge from the ordeal of rejection with the knowledge that it won't stop them. As painful as it may be, a rejection is only one person's reaction and not the final, game-ending buzzer.

Often, among the debris of rejection, you find nuggets of information that light the way to a stronger revision. It's hard, but if you accept that what you sent out the first time wasn't perfect, the combination of the feedback you've received and the passage of time that allows you to approach the manuscript with fresh eyes gives you insight into things that may be improved.

And most important of all, now you understand the true nature of the conflict and what it will take to see it through to the *Final Battle*.

THE ROAD BACK

In its tenth phase, the pace of the hero's journey quickens as, armed with the hard-won *Reward*, the hero embarks on *The Road Back* that leads inevitably to the *Final Battle*.

The critical opening of this phase is the determination, made in the full knowledge of what the hero has suffered and of what the antagonist is capable, to go back and fight again. This time, the hero must not simply survive but triumph in order to keep the ordinary world of his village safe. Armed with *The Reward*, the hero knows he has the means to defeat the villain. He also knows that the price of failure will be his own destruction.

But the road back is not an easy one. The antagonist throws everything he has at the hero, erecting one impossible obstacle after another. From the hero's perspective, it seems as though heaven and hell are conspiring against him, testing his resolve every step of the way back to the *Final Battle*.

As a writer, one aspect of *The Road Back* is a determination to keep submitting with the full knowledge that you're setting yourself up for more rejection. Another, and perhaps more important, aspect is to keep writing, with faith that your hard-won knowledge will make your work better.

But you must be prepared because your road back will also be filled with obstacles that test your resolve.

Unlike the hero's journey in stories, the pace of your real-life journey will not pick up in this phase. Indeed, you may feel that things are slowing down. What you'll find is that you spend a lot of time cycling between *Ordeal*, *Reward*, and *The Road Back* because final confrontations that irrevocably change things one way or another are rare except in fiction.

The one thing, though, that is true in both stories and life, is that the hero always keeps going.

THE FINAL BATTLE AND RESURRECTION

At the climax of the hero's journey, in its mythic form, the hero challenges and defeats the greatest antagonist of all: death. In this last great conflict, the hero descends to the darkest pit, subdues the foe, and rises above it all, resurrected, either literally or figuratively, as a new, transcendent man.

In contemporary storytelling, we generally think in terms of a final, decisive confrontation. Everything is at stake in the *Final Battle*. The hero will either triumph or be destroyed, along with everything he holds dear. The resolution of this conflict changes everything, most particularly the hero.

As real and final as the stakes are, the theme is actually transcendence and transformation: like a rite of passage, the journey, particularly its culmination, changes the hero into a new person. That change mirrors the larger change in the world brought about by the antagonist's defeat.

Of course in our day of superabundant media, writing a book rarely changes everyone's world. But like the hero's *Final Battle*, seeing your project through to its conclusion (which may or may not involve publication) can change your world. While there may be external changes, like a publishing contract, the ones that really matter are internal: in ways large and small, this process has transformed you.

RETURN WITH THE ELIXIR

After all the excitement of the *Final Battle* and the hero's transcendent victory, the last stage of the hero's journey, in which he *Returns with the Elixir*, may feel like an obligatory dénouement.

In many stories, the return is a cause for celebration and/or a wedding—something to show that balance and peace have been restored.

You may be tempted to dismiss it as a bit of a formality. In fact, many movies end with the dawning of a new day (either figuratively or literally) after the antagonist has been defeated, confident that the audience understands that everything will be well now.

But there's an important dimension to the return that you mustn't overlook: it is the proof of the hero's transformation.

Take, for example, the hobbits' return to the Shire after all their adventures across Middle Earth and in the War of the Ring. Instead of the furtive four who barely made it to Bree without Strider's protection, Frodo, Sam, Merry, and Pippin (along with the hobbits who rally round the heroes) are more than a match for the ruffians who had taken over their homes.

And what about you, as a writer?

How has the journey transformed you?

What will you do with your hard-won power and knowledge?

RETROSPECT

The hero's journey was most succinctly characterized by Bilbo Baggins when he titled his memoirs (which we know as **The Hobbit**), "There and Back Again."

Because of the overriding urgency of the impending crisis that impels the hero to undertake the journey, we tend to think of a linear progression from problem, through attempts and failings, to the ultimate solution. When painting with broad brushes, we use the quest as a task-oriented synonym for the hero's journey: obtain the goal or meet the conditions of the quest and you're done.

In doing so, we lose sight of the fact that the hero's journey is a mythic cycle.

Myth is not history. History is what happened in a particular time and place. Myth is what happened, what is happening, and what will happen in many times and places.

And the important thing about the pattern is that it is a cycle: the hero's journey is really about coming full circle.

Consider the outbound and inbound parallels:

It begins in the *The Ordinary World* and ends there when the hero *Returns with the Elixir. Called to Adventure,* the hero *Refuses the Call* because of fear—the very fears he must confront in the **Final Battle** and transcend in his *Resurrection* as a new man. One or more *Mentors* help the hero *Cross the Threshold* into the unknown world, just as hard-won *Rewards* give the hero the knowledge and the wherewithal to take *The Road Back* that leads to the *Final Battle*. The middle of the journey is about discovering *Allies and Enemies*, attempting to resolve the crisis by *Approaching the In-most Cave*, and enduring *Ordeals*.

This all may seem overly academic.

Why can't we just say, "Stuff happens," and be satisfied?

Because when there's a recurring pattern, stuff isn't simply happening. The twelve phases of the hero's journey are not simply labels that Joseph Campbell found convenient for his purposes. Each represents a potential point of failure in the arc of character development:

The Ordinary World

- If the hero is too comfortable, there is no journey.

- If writers are too comfortable, they never start their projects.

The Call to Adventure

- If nothing threatens the village, there is no need for the hero to undertake the journey.

- If writers never have a moment of inspiration—no, "Hey, I could write a book," epiphany—there's no need to actually write.

Refusing the Call

- If the threat is easily dismissed, there is no need for a hero.

- If the idea is only strong enough for a blog post or an essay, there is no need to write a book.

Mentors

- Without guidance, would-be heroes flounder and fail.
- Without guidance (or at least support and some kind of positive feedback), new writers generally flounder until their enthusiasm for the project wanes.

Crossing the Threshold

- If the hero stays with the mentor, to prepare a bit more or hone another skill, and never sets out on the journey proper, the village will not be saved.
- If writers are forever studying the craft, keeping up with the industry, going to conferences, taking courses, participating in critique groups, and all the dozens of ways in which one can feel like a writer without actually writing, their book will never be finished.

Allies and Enemies

- If the hero fails to distinguish between the allies and enemies he encounters in the special world, his journey will end badly.
- If writers don't know who to trust, if they follow bad advice, or get impatient and rush to market, their effort to create and promote a book will end badly.

Approaching the In-most Cave

- If the hero never attempts to carry the fight to the enemy, he'll never learn what he needs to know or acquire the item that will make the difference in the final battle.

- If writers never put their work out for others to see, they'll never learn about their strengths and weaknesses or who their audience is and what resonates with them.

Ordeals

- If the hero succumbs to the ordeal or loses his nerve, he fails.

- If writers are overwhelmed by rejection and withdraw, they fail.

Rewards

- If the hero fails to claim the reward for surviving the ordeal or the hard-won knowledge it has to offer, he will not have what he needs to win in the final battle.

- If writers don't learn from and grow stronger through rejections, they'll stand no chance against the merciless one-star reviewers who will pounce on their books.

The Road Back

- If the hero turns aside from the road back to the final confrontation, the battle is over before it begins.

- If, in the seemingly endless rounds of revisions, writers lose faith, interest, or even the vision that carried them to this point, the book will die before it's been born.

The Final Battle and Resurrection

- If the hero isn't transformed by the final conflict—if he doesn't transcend his foes—he will win, at best, a hollow victory and stands a good chance of becoming the new enemy.

- If writers don't transcend the painful, grinding process of publication, and find a pure and unsullied joy in their work, they will go down a path of bitterness and cynicism, in which writing becomes a Sisyphean chore.

Return with the Elixir

- If the hero doesn't return with the elixir, the village will not be made whole and the hero betrays everything for which he has suffered and fought.

- If writer never give back to the readers, to the writing community, or even to themselves and those nearest and dearest, they are headed for irrelevancy, perhaps even ruin.

It is no accident that Campbell discovered the archetype of the hero's journey in myths from around the world because it happens all the time. You have likely had and will have experiences that more or less follow this pattern—though you probably wouldn't call them heroic because they involve much smaller stakes. By the same token, as your characters grow and change over the course of your story, the pattern of the hero's journey can add verisimilitude to their transformations.

CHAPTER 24.

THE VIRGIN'S PROMISE

Kim Hudson, in **The Virgin's Promise** [6], worked out the feminine counterpart of the hero's journey.

> "Although they are both stories about learning to stand alone, the Virgin story is about knowing her dream for herself and bringing it to life while surrounded by the influences of her kingdom. The Hero story is about facing mortal danger by leaving his village and proving he can exist in a larger world. The Virgin shifts her values over the course of her story to fully be herself in the world. The Hero is focused on developing his skills to actively do things that need to be done in the world. The Virgin is about self-fulfillment while the Hero is about self-sacrifice."

There are thirteen phases in the arc of the realization of the virgin's promise:

The Dependent World: we see the world upon which the virgin is dependent and in which she has a predetermined role.

The Price of Conformity: we see how the virgin suppresses her true self to conform to the wishes of those around her and get a glimpse of what could happen if she doesn't conform.

Opportunity to Shine: through accident or oversight the virgin stumbles into a situation in which she discovers or reveals some of her potential.

Dresses the Part: the virgin tests the possibility that her dream might be realized by figuratively or literally trying it on in a joyful burst of exploration.

The Secret World: the virgin creates a secret place in which to nurture her dream.

No Longer Fits Her World: as the virgin grows more confident in her dream, the tension of juggling the secret and dependent worlds grows as well.

Caught Shining: the virgin's secret and dependent worlds collide when she is discovered acting outside her appointed role.

Gives Up What Kept Her Stuck: faced with censure (or worse) the virgin gives up the attachments to her dependent world that kept her torn between it and her dream.

The Kingdom in Chaos: the virgin's actions upset the order of the dependent world, which rallies its forces to bring her back into conformity.

Wanders in the Wilderness: doubting herself because of the chaos in the kingdom, the virgin's convictions are tested and she's tempted to repent and return to her dependent world.

Chooses her Light: the virgin chooses her dream—"She would rather shine than be safe."

The Reordering (Rescue): the virgin's dependent world is

reordered (sometimes forcibly) and recognizes her value when she lives as her true self.

The Kingdom is Brighter: because of the virgin's challenge and the consequent reordering of her world, everyone is better off.

The gender associated with the hero's journey and the virgin's promise is a matter of common experience, not necessity: men and women can go through both patterns at different times and places in their lives. The determining factor is whether you are already a part of a community and enmeshed in its web of expectations or whether you must leave your community and make your way in the world.

THE DEPENDENT WORLD

The arc of the virgin's promise, like the hero's journey, begins in a community. But where the hero must leave the community in order to protect it, the virgin's growth and self-discovery takes place within the community. Where the hero is motivated by a belief that the community is worth preserving, the virgin's story begins in a community so intent on preserving its ways that it has woven a web of constricting expectations around her. This web has the effect, whether intended or not, of keeping the virgin dependent and compliant.

The young, those who have too little (or too much), and those who are socially isolated depend on others for physical survival. The virgin may depend on some people to protect her from others in her society. She may be in a situation where the love she needs depends on her conformity. Many societies have developed attitudes, mores, and conventions that enforce dependence because they, in turn, depend upon the affected people to fulfill their roles and conform to expectations. Women, for example, often have the primary responsibility for transmitting culture and traditions to the next generation. Such societies usually have powerful sanctions to keep women from taking on roles that would interfere with the transmission process.

It is almost always the case that the virgin's dependent world is not so much malevolent as constricting. The community doesn't need to be overthrown, just adjusted. Put another way, much of the inner conflict the virgin suffers during her transformation arises precisely because she doesn't want to sacrifice the good in her dependent world.

As a writer, you are likely past the stage in life where you depended directly on others. You may, however, have dependents. The people in your world probably depend on you not writing: whether breadwinner or caregiver, none of those who depend upon you will think the prospect of you spending thousands of hours putting words on paper with no guarantee of a return instead of paying attention to them is a good idea.

And for your part, spending your time and attention on the people who depend on you is a good thing because the community and your relationships in it matter to you. But before you were Mom or Dad, you were someone else. And while you love being Mom or Dad, that's not the sum and substance of your identity. And yet you're surrounded by voices, most of them well-meaning, who leave you feeling guilty that you're not doing enough.

If this rings true, congratulations: you understand the constraining complexity of the *Dependent World* and the beginning of the arc of the virgin's promise.

THE PRICE OF CONFORMITY

The *Dependent World*, that is the world upon which the virgin is dependent, provides for her needs. The price for this is conformity, specifically conforming to the expectations of others.

Conformity is not necessarily a bad thing. It is, in fact, the foundation of civil society. Conforming, for example, to traffic rules allows us to travel the roads and highways at will and in relative safety. But as with many things, where a little conformity is a good thing, too much is bad. As Hudson explains:

> "The Price of Conformity is the suppression of the Virgin's true self. When the Virgin subscribes to the views of the people around her, she experiences a loss of self. Even when she is aware of what she wants, she doesn't see how she could achieve it."

You might conform because of ignorance or an uncritical acceptance of the situation. (Hudson calls this, "sleeping through her life.") You might understand but still agree to conform because you see no other or better option. You might conform because you're too focused on meeting the needs of others.

"Often girls are highly praised for being helpful, beautiful, and thoughtful to others," Hudson says. "The Virgin is soon so busy meeting the needs of others that there is little time or room to discover her own needs."

How often have you heard someone say, "I once thought I'd do or make or become something, but then life came along ..." or, "I wanted to study art, but my father insisted I study accounting."

None of us, of course, is entitled to have all our dreams fulfilled. But none of us should have to go through life without fulfilling a single dream. This is the scope of the *Price of Conformity*.

At this point, you might say, "It's obvious that the *Price of Conformity* for writers is not writing." There clearly are many people who read a book, think, "Oh, I could do better than that," and yet because of the relentless pressure of the *Dependent World* never get around to stringing words together.

But what most people infected by the dream of the scribbler want is not just to write but to write what they want to write. There's a more subtle, yet far greater, price to be paid for conformity if you never get to write what you want. You may claim to have realized your dream if you find a job that involves writing or even establish yourself as a writer, but so long as you are compelled to write what others expect you to write, you haven't escaped the *Price of Conformity*.

OPPORTUNITY TO SHINE

We say that a story should start with an inciting incident—something which changes the protagonist's world enough that it's impossible for them to continue with business as usual.

The inciting incident in the arc of the virgin's promise is the *Opportunity to Shine*. Whether because she was in the right place at the right time, found a place to try something while no one was looking, or had to step up because someone was in need, the *Opportunity to Shine* is the first intimation that the Virgin might do more than simply conform to everyone else's expectations: she reveals a talent, dream, or heretofore suppressed aspect of her true nature.

There are several important distinctions between the virgin's *Opportunity to Shine* and the hero's *Call to Adventure*, the inciting incident in each cycle.

First, the inciting incident comes later for the virgin. The *Call to Adventure* is the second beat in the hero's journey, while the *Opportunity to Shine* is the third beat in the virgin's promise. The motivation for the hero is straightforward: something threatens the wellbeing of the village and someone needs to do something about it. The situation for the virgin is more complex. There is much about her *Dependent World* that is worth preserving, but she's weighed down by the *Price of Conformity*. With the *Opportunity to Shine*, the virgin discovers she might have alternatives. This slower start is important because we can't appreciate the virgin's *Opportunity to Shine* if we don't understand her world and what it costs her to live there.

A second, and critical difference, is that unlike the hero, whose inciting incident involves an explicit threat, the virgin isn't trying to change her world. She steps up and shines precisely because doing so doesn't (or doesn't appear to) threaten her world. The virgin's motive is opposite that of the hero.

Many writers follow a similar path to writing. Perhaps it's a brochure for a volunteer organization, a report at work, or a story for a program at the library. You certainly wouldn't call yourself a writer, but someone needed help or there was an opportunity to give it a whirl. Then people took notice. They said your words made a difference. And you began to think this may not have been a one-off thing.

DRESSES THE PART

Thanks to the industrial revolution, which started in textiles and put us on a course to cheap and abundant clothing, we moderns have a weak appreciation of the power of dress. From days playing dress up as children to actors who become the character as they put on their costume and make up, what we wear and how we adorn ourselves has long had the power to transform us from naked apes into, say, an officer or lady of the court.

In *Dresses the Part*, having awakened to the possibility of something more in the *Opportunity to Shine*, the virgin now tries on the role, sometimes literally.

Clothing, because it is such an integral and intimate part of our experience, is potent on both practical and symbolic levels. It can be an enabler or an impediment; it can empower or constrict. So both dressing and undressing can be the prelude to exploration.

Of course, this talk of clothing doesn't preclude stories where the enabler is some other object, situation, or concept. The key (sometimes an actual key) is that the virgin now has the opportunity to explore her dream in a safe, non-threatening context.

In the visual vocabulary of film, this beat is often shown in montage as a kind of fashion show during which the virgin tries to find the right fit for her growing possibilities.

A consequence of *Dressing the Part* is that the Virgin becomes beautiful—perhaps not all at once, or not in ways that are immediately apparent, but in ways that reflect her internal transformation. As Hudson explains:

"... true beauty is seen when the soul of a person is reflected in their physical appearance.... The Virgin's beauty is often described in terms of light such as shining, glowing, brilliant, dazzling, and iridescent. In other words, the Virgin's beauty represents the shining forth of her soul."

Stories often highlight this transformation by showing the Virgin as something of an ugly duckling at the beginning.

It's important to remember that the beauty we're discussing here has nothing to do with the community's definitions or expectations about beauty. This is not the sculpted and manicured beauty of a fashion model, but the natural beauty of a person full of life and vitality.

Dressing the part as a writer has little to do with actual clothing. Nor do you need special equipment—purchasing a computer is far less significant, because of its multiple uses, than buying a typewriter once was for a writer. But you do need to explore both subjects and disciplines to find the right fit.

Trying different subjects, and by extension, addressing different audiences is the writing analogue of the fashion show. What kind of stories do you enjoy? What kind of writing fires your passion? To which of your pieces do people respond most strongly?

Writing discipline is the less glamorous but ultimately more important aspect of *Dressing the Part* for writers. Questions like when to write and whether to have music in the background are expressions of a deeper, primal fear: can I really do this, not just today but for the long run?

The only way to really know you can sustain the effort over an entire career is to sustain the effort over an entire career. All authors, even the most successful, wonder if they can keep it up; if the next book will be as successful as the last; if people still want to listen. That said, by dressing the part (i.e., treating your writing like a profession) you can learn a great deal about how realistic your dream may be and, more importantly, how well it fits your soul and brings out your inner beauty.

THE SECRET WORLD

The idea that a superhero must have a secret identity is so firmly established it's well past cliché and on its way to becoming a *Law of Nature*. There is, of course, the practical matter of not giving the super villains a target when you need some down time. But at a basic psychological level, there's something powerful and invigorating in having a secret.

Hudson explains the role of the *Secret World* in the arc of the virgin's promise:

> "She's not ready to reveal her dream to her Dependent World and face the consequences. The Virgin goes back and forth, juggling the impulse to meet the expectations of her Dependent World with creating a separate and Secret World where she can grow into herself."

A *Secret World* may be a place, a time, or simply an idea. It's generally something overlooked or ignored by the *Dependent World*—like the secret garden, in Frances Hodgson Burnett's book of the same name, which was literally beneath the notice of the housekeeper. In fact, it's critical that the *Secret World* is something that the *Dependent World* believes is inconsequential: if they suspect anything else they'll shut down the virgin's explorations before she can threaten the complex of expectations placed upon her.

This is not to say that the *Secret World* must always be something benign and inoffensive. The virgin may be doing something that would unsettle her *Dependent World*, during a time when their attention is elsewhere.

The joy of exploring what's possible in the *Secret World* is colored—and perhaps heightened—by the fear of discovery, where discovery could mean anything from the death of the dream to an actual death sentence in more restrictive societies.

Again, unlike the hero who sets out to confront problems directly, in the arc of the virgin's promise it's important to be clear that the virgin's motive is self-realization and that she actively avoids conflict, particularly with her *Dependent World*, during the initial stages of the arc.

Another key part of this phase is that the virgin believes she can please everyone, including herself. This is how she justifies exploring her dreams and the possibilities in the *Secret World*.

As a writer, it's easy to believe you can please everyone—you can be a star employee, a sterling partner and/or parent, and knock out a novel without breaking a sweat.

Some of you may be shaking your heads at that last sentence. In the cold light of rationality, we would all agree you can't do everything.

The cold light of rationality, however, doesn't shine on the *Secret World* because it is fundamentally irrational—not in the sense of madness but in the simpler sense that one can't make a rational evaluation with incomplete information. The *Secret World* is full of new possibilities, including the possibility of pleasing everyone. After all, wouldn't the people who depend on you be pleased if your novel brought them fame and fortune?

This phase is particularly seductive for a writer because you have not one but two *Secret Worlds* into which you can retire. The first is the role of the writer: you go from being mild-mannered, Responsible-Person by day to sparkling, witty, Writer-Person by night. The second, more consuming seduction, is the secret world of the story, where for a time, with a heady mix of god-like power and child-like wonder, you are the only one making footprints in the snow.

NO LONGER FITS HER WORLD

At a macro level, economists tell us it's the only real answer to our financial problems. At a micro level, an endless parade of self-help gurus each promise us the secret to personal growth.

There's much less discussion of the consequences of growth. Regardless of the scale, whether populations and economies or waistlines, unchecked growth in a finite context means we will inevitable get too big for our britches.

The virgin's promise captures a pattern of personal growth. The inevitable consequence of exploring possibilities in *Dresses the Part* and nurturing her dream in her *Secret World* is that the virgin grows and comes to realize she *No Longer Fits Her World*. Growing toward her dream creates a tension with her *Dependent World* that she finds increasingly difficult to balance.

In dramatic terms, because the virgin *No Longer Fits Her World*, she inevitably does something that puts either her *Dependent World* or her *Secret World* at risk. It may be as simple as deciding the task of achieving her dream is too hard and her *Dependent World* isn't that bad after all. Or, at the other end of the spectrum she may find her dream within her grasp and be frightened by the prospect of losing her *Dependent World*. The virgin may also become reckless or attract attention in some other way.

Whether the source of the dramatic tension is internal or external, it is a direct consequence of the virgin's growth.

As a writer, particularly if your efforts have met with some success, you will inevitably reach the point where you feel as though you've outgrown both your dependent and secret worlds. The siren song of the full-time writer is the single greatest temptation: think of how much more you could accomplish if you didn't have to divide your time with a day job.

If you're struggling with that temptation, step back and take a deep breath. In the vast majority of cases, it would be reckless to quit your day job. But beyond good advice, as someone who can see the entire arc of a story, you should recognize that you're going through a stage similar to this phase in the virgin's promise. The tension you feel between the safety of your old world and the alluring possibilities of the new writing world is exactly what you should be feeling.

Of course, saying it doesn't make it any easier, but perhaps if you recognize the structural source of your concern you can at least avoid doing anything rash.

CAUGHT SHINING

"Too good to last," is the weaker corollary of, "too good to be true." In structural terms, if a thing is unsustainable something must give. You may be able to study or work all day and party all night once or twice, but if you keep it up something like your health, an important relationship, or a critical responsibility will fall apart.

This phase is the inevitable consequence of the virgin's attempt to balance her *Dependent World* and her *Secret World*. The tensions that built during *No Longer Fits Her World* snap, catapulting her in to the very conflicts she worked so hard to avoid.

In *Caught Shining*, the virgin's secret world is revealed. The catalyst behind her revelation may simply be the consequence of the virgin's growth. Or the circumstances that created the space for her *Secret World* may change. Sometimes others act to expose her *Secret World*. Someone from her *Dependent World* may recognize her, or a confidant may betray her.

Whatever the cause, this phase overflows with conflict. Because conflict is precisely what the virgin has been trying to avoid, this point in the arc of the virgin's promise takes her to the nadir of the cycle. Analogous to *The Ordeal* in the hero's journey, it is the beginning of her darkest times.

The more cynical scribblers may say, "Been there, done that—if you're a writer, it's definitional."

It does seem that writers are peculiarly susceptible to self-doubt (though it may be that we suffer no more angst than is common to mortals, it's just that we're better at expressing it), but the emotional ordeal of this phase in the arc is deeper: it challenges everything you thought you were becoming—either directly or by alleging damage to your dependent world.

You may be accused of neglecting your family, your job, or your future. You may be charged with making the people you care about suffer for your vanity. Or you may simply run into the realization that you have nothing more to show for all your efforts than a drawer full of abandoned manuscripts and rejections.

It's a time of questions and no answers.

GIVES UP WHAT KEPT HER STUCK

At the end of the last phase, the virgin's temporary balance between her dependent and secret worlds had fallen apart. Now the only way to escape from the wreckage is for something else to give: the virgin must *Give up What Kept Her Stuck.*

One of the key steps at the beginning of the arc of the virgin's promise is to establish the *Price of Conformity*. It is critical to establish that context because the drama in this phase is driven by the virgin's realization, because of what she has become, that the price of conformity is now too great. But, beset by fears that she might be hurt or no longer loved if she follows her own path, that knowledge isn't sufficient to move her forward.

When the virgin finally musters the courage to act, the moment is cathartic: all the old limitations melt away and she finds herself in a world of possibilities—real possibilities, far greater in scope than those in the *Secret World*. The energy locked in the old complex of expectations is released and gives the virgin the strength to go forward.

Like the virgin, often it is the web of expectations woven around you that keep you stuck. From the obvious expectations that you meet your daily obligations instead of dropping everything to write, to the more subtle but ultimately more debilitating expectations you have of your writing—that it has to be a bestseller or secure a large advance—you force your words and your efforts to craft those words to carry far more than their fair share of expectations.

Those expectations are often the root cause of writer's block: the fear that your writing is not good enough is really the fear that your writing isn't suitable for some predetermined purpose. It's no accident that remedies for writers block generally involve writing something that is explicitly useless: it's a way to give up what is keeping you stuck.

After reading that last sentence, you may be tempted to put on your snark and say, "Well, duh. Give up what keeps you stuck? That's why it's called, 'Writers block.'"

That's an astute observation, even though you thought you were being snide. Your frustration—"Of course I would give up what's keeping me stuck if I knew what it was!"—is an important part of the Virgin's emotional turmoil during this phase. Think about your own bouts with writer's block and how in retrospect you knew what you needed to do but couldn't or wouldn't for a time.

Think, too, about how you felt when you got past the block: the burst of joy, perhaps even borderline euphoria, as the words—good words—began to flow.

Those are the feelings you need to channel as you write your protagonist through the arc of the virgin's promise. And those are the feelings you need to treasure and have ready to call upon for encouragement when you can't move forward until you give up what is keeping you stuck.

THE KINGDOM IN CHAOS

One of the things that set us apart, as a species, is our ability to recognize patterns—or, more to the point, our ability to detect patterns and variations. We instantly notice when something, or someone, is out of line.

Stepping out of line is precisely what the virgin did in the previous phase, *Gives up What Kept Her Stuck*. Now, what had been a private struggle becomes public as others in her *Dependent World* notice and react to the virgin's choice. The spreading confusion in this phase leaves the *Kingdom in Chaos*.

What was a private transformation is now manifest in public. People form opinions and take sides. Questions and conflicts perturb the sense of order.

Whether the virgin's actions are the direct cause of or only a catalyst for simmering tensions that existed in the kingdom before she was *Caught Shining*, the forces of order and stability react—and sometimes overreact—in an effort to bring the virgin back into line.

If conflict is the narrative fuel, this is the point where the story's afterburners kick in. While there are ample opportunities for external conflict, complete with violence and physical coercion, the realization of the fears she discovered in *No Longer Fits Her World*, and the attendant burden of guilt, throws the Virgin into an internal conflict that is as bad as or worse than the external situation.

A writer can face a kingdom in chaos at a number of levels. Perhaps breaking out of your writer's block, or a revision letter from an editor, leaves your manuscript in chaos. Perhaps an unbreakable stream of rejections leaves your plan to work toward publication (and realize your dreams) in chaos. Perhaps life intrudes and leaves your efforts to write in chaos.

When it seems as though the universe is conspiring against you, the fears you can never banish will rear up and confront you with your own inadequacy: you're a fraud, you know it, and it would be best for everyone if you gave up this writing nonsense and went back to where you were safe and comfortable.

It's not pretty and it's not fun, but these are the emotional depths you must plumb in order to capture the dramatic crux of the virgin's struggle to realize her promise.

WANDERS IN THE WILDERNESS

The ancient religious sanction of excommunication carries far less weight than it once did. In our complex society, with its layers of real and virtual social networks, it's easy to find a new community when we leave (or are thrown out of) an old one. There was a time, however, when being cast out was tantamount to a death sentence.

The inevitable consequence of the virgin's bid for independence, which leaves the *Kingdom in Chaos*, is that she suffers the ultimate sanction in the *Dependent World* and is excommunicated by the agents trying to restore order. This forces the virgin, whether figuratively or literally, to *Wander in the Wilderness*.

Like *The Ordeal* in the hero's journey, *Wandering in the Wilderness* is the virgin's near death experience—the test of all she thinks she has become. But as a social death she has the option to go back to the *Dependent World*, conform, and make everyone except herself happy. Where the hero faces life or death, the virgin chooses between kinds of life. Determining how you will die says a lot about your character. Determining how you will live says more.

Because it is a solitary pursuit, writers often wander in the wilderness: every time you share your work and get a reaction other than the one you expected, you have reason to doubt yourself. During a time when you get nothing but rejections—if you get any response at all—you have to wonder if the crazy one in this relationship might actually be you and not the world.

Like the aphorism that character is what you do when no one is looking, the way you handle those times when you wander in the wilderness speaks volumes about who you are and whether you have the stamina and strength of character to stand the test of time that is the author's vocation.

CHOOSES HER LIGHT

Stories are fundamentally about choices and consequences. There are, of course, highly praised novels that show the meaninglessness of existence, but the vast majority of stories are about people who choose and do—even if it is a mistake. This is why one common way to talk about story structure is in terms of try-fail cycles.

The eleventh phase of the virgin's promise, *Chooses Her Light*, is the point where the virgin chooses to let the light of her true self shine and acts accordingly. Trusting herself, and determined to stay true to her dream, this is the moment of joyous transformation, analogous to *The Resurrection* in the hero's journey.

Because of the chaos in the kingdom, she was banished by the forces trying to restore order to the *Dependent World* to *Wander in the Wilderness* until she repented. *Choosing Her Light* is neither capitulating to the forces of order nor giving up on herself. It is the moment in which the virgin transcends her *Dependent World*, and in so doing gains the power to act and not be acted upon.

It is critical that the virgin acts for herself—that she is the prime mover in this phase. Even if her actions place her in danger and she needs help, she's the one moving everything forward. The core of the transformation that comes with *Chooses Her Light* is that the virgin finally harnesses and harmonizes her inner desires and outward actions in order to realize her dream.

Hudson uses the metaphor of going to a ball as a radiant beauty to characterize the way in which the virgin introduces her true form to the kingdom.

For writers, the opportunities to stand out in your kingdom in all your authorial splendor are few and far between. It's nearly impossible to come out as a writer as a prelude to living happily ever after because no matter how lovely last night's ball might have been, there's always a blank page awaiting you in the cold light of dawn.

It is the choosing that resonates most strongly with the writer's experience: after wandering in your own personal wildernesses, you choose your light as a writer and take clear and concrete action to move toward your dreams—the clearest and most concrete of which is to put your words down on the page, and then to do it again tomorrow.

RE-ORDERING (RESCUE)

At the end of the stereotypical western, the hero rides off into the sunset: the town is now safe from the desperadoes, and there are other wrongs elsewhere that need righting.

The arc of the virgin's promise never ends this way. As much as it seems to be the story of the Virgin coming into her own as an individual and making a place for herself in her community, it is also a story about the way in which the virgin heals her community. The hero averts an external threat and his job is done when the village can once again sleep safely. The virgin had to undergo her transformation because of forces internal to the community and she hasn't addressed the real problem if she simply walks away. Even though her personal development culminates in the previous beat, *Chooses Her Light*, the story of her community isn't over until it passes through the *Re-ordering (Rescue)* phase.

The community that dismissed, vilified, or banished the Virgin in an attempt to make her conform to the *Dependent World* now acknowledges her value—that she has more to offer when she *Chooses Her Light* than she would by conforming to the expectations of her *Dependent World*.

This is not simply a grudging admission that the virgin many have had a point. The social malignancy that created the original problem for the virgin must be addressed in order to reconnect her with her kingdom.

The process of reconnecting the virgin with her kingdom is not a trivial one. The kingdom as a whole must transform. If the forces of the old order resist the re-ordering, particularly if they focus on the virgin as their antagonist, she may be in danger of being destroyed. As Hudson explains:

"It is not the nature of the Virgin to assert her will over the will of others. She inspires others to change out of love or a drive towards joy. The Hero, on the other hand, does assert his will against evil."

It is critical that the *Re-ordering (rescue)* recognizes the Virgin's worth and reconnects her with her community. A rescue that accomplishes only one of those aims is a false one. Reconnecting the virgin with her community without recognizing her worth is nothing more than capitulating to her *Dependent World*. A rescue that recognizes her worth but places her in another community simply replaces her old *Dependent World* with a new one. Stories often tempt the virgin with false rescues, but thanks to her transformation, she now sees them for what they are.

Seeing things for what they are is also critical to your development as a writer. You start with dreams that are the literary equivalent of the girl in the chorus line who catches the producer's eye and is whisked away to stardom, with an agent getting you great deals, editors polishing your award-winning prose, and sales people putting you on the bestsellers list.

Notice, though, how passive the object of all the attention is in these dreams. Like the arc of the virgin's promise, in order to establish yourself as an individual who has a valued place in the community you must act and not simply be acted upon. This will mean different things for different writers, but they will all have the general character of doing things for motives that flow from you and not because of externally imposed expectations. For example, you will not write because you hope to catch the next market wave but because you have a story you want to tell.

THE KINGDOM IS BRIGHTER

The best atmospheric metaphor for the culmination of the virgin's promise is a sunrise: the dark night has ended and the day begins with renewed life and energy. At the end of the arc, parallel to and catalyzed by the virgin's personal transformation, *The Kingdom is Brighter* because the community has also chosen its own light.

The Virgin doesn't ride off into the sunset, as we discussed in the last section, because the problem all along was internal to her community. While the arc of the virgin's promise is, at one level, a story of coming into one's own as an individual, it is also about doing so in the context of a community—one that is neither wholly good nor bad. And as the virgin had to stretch and grow and make a new place for herself to break free from the web of expectations that kept her from realizing her dreams, so too did the kingdom: whether because of complacency, traditions growing rigid, or a festering social evil, the kingdom was also trapped and unable to realize the dream of its potential.

Like curtains thrown open to flood a room with the crisp light of a new day, in this final phase the kingdom blossoms with new life—figuratively and sometimes literally. More importantly, now that the social malignancy has been healed, there is an outpouring, at least in the virgin's immediate circle, of unconditional love.

The beautiful thing about coming to the end of a satisfying and well-told story is that we're left to savor that final, perfect image. Life outside of the story has a tendency of marring a perfect, culminating moment through the simple fact that it goes on. The morning after you receive the Nobel Prize for Literature you'll still have to get up, get dressed, and do something useful.

I can't enumerate all the ways in which your kingdom will be brighter as you realize your writing dreams. But I can tell you that light is a fleeting thing. If you don't fix it in your memory, the time will come when no one remembers how bright the kingdom was.

But rather than despairing that it didn't last, take inspiration from the hope that what once was may be again: for one brief, shining moment, there really was a Camelot.

And in a larger sense, this is why the Virgin's Promise and the Hero's Journey are archetypes: these are stories that are always unfolding. Coming to the end of one cycle means that soon we will begin another.

LOOKING BACK

We've come a long way as we've followed the arc of the virgin's promise. You might be tempted to say it's only the story of someone in a community who, constrained by a web of expectations, finds a way to grow into their dream, make a new place for themselves, and make the community better in the process. But that's both too curt and dismissive.

First, like the hero's journey, the phases in the arc of the virgin's promise are each significant because each represents a failure point—that is, a test of character where a different decision brings an end to personal growth and returns the protagonists to their *Dependent World*. The personal transformation in both cases requires courage, determination, and stamina but in very different ways. While the hero faces an antagonist who is evil because his actions threaten the village, the Virgin faces antagonists who are good, or at least well intentioned. Even if the Kingdom suffers from a festering evil, the Virgin is only in danger after she exposes and challenges that evil. The hero's courage to persevere in the face of a life-or-death threat is very different from the virgin's courage to persevere in the face of well-meaning people who want her to accept her place in the community because they believe it's the best way to make the most people happy.

Second, like all stories of real change, the process involves a number of necessary steps. In any given case, a person going through the transformation may move quickly from one particular phase to another, but you short-circuit the transformation if you skip too many steps. Take the simpler example of grief: going from denial straight to acceptance means you didn't actually grieve. So too, if the virgin goes from *Opportunity to Shine* to the *Kingdom is Brighter* it means that the web of expectations wasn't that constricting after all and you don't really have a story.

The necessity of the majority of the phases in the arc is clearer if we map the phases into a three-act structure.

Introduction (Establishing Context)

- The Dependent World
- The Price of Conformity
- Opportunity to Shine (the Inciting Incident)

Act I (first try/fail cycle)

- Dresses the Part

- The Secret World
- No Longer Fits Her World
- Caught Shining (First Failure)

Act II (second try/fail cycle)

- Gives up What Kept Her Stuck
- The Kingdom in Chaos
- Wanders in the Wilderness (Second Failure)

Act III (final try/succeed cycle)

- Chooses Her Light
- Re-ordering (Rescue)
- The Kingdom is Brighter (resolution)

It is, however, not simply a matter of trying three times. The transformation occurs through the process of trying, growing, and failing in each cycle. Put another way, the virgin in the given an *Opportunity to Shine* phase is capable of taking the small steps that bring her to the *Secret World* where she has a safe place to grow, but would wither if thrown immediately into the challenges of *Wanders in the Wilderness*.

So what does it mean?

Beyond the obvious application to fictional character development, there are lessons for your own development, both as a writer and as an individual.

Perhaps the most important lesson for both life and fiction is that true change is neither quick nor easy. There is no growth without pain. It may be the acute pain of direct conflict or the chronic pain of a transformation that comes only through a long, slow process.

Moreover, failure is not only common but necessary to the process. That this is so is clearer in the arc of the virgin's promise because her goal, particularly through *Caught Shining*, is not to change her world but simply to make a better place in it for herself. Her failure to balance the increasingly conflicting demands forces her out of the places that are comfortable and safe into new territory where she must discover and draw upon resources she never knew she had.

Knowing these things won't make your cycles of growth less painful. But in recognizing them, you can take solace in the knowledge, even as you *Wander in the Wilderness*, that you're not alone and that if you find the hidden reservoirs of strength to stay true to your dream the *Kingdom will be Brighter*.

CHAPTER 25.

ROMANCE

An artist, a banker, and an engineer were discussing wives and mistresses over lunch.

"I will never marry," the artist declared. "The passion, the longing, and the mystery of an affair—this is what powers my work."

The banker shook his head. "Nonsense. Stability, not to mention the tax advantages, make a wife the best choice."

"I always have both," the engineer said.

"How can this be?" the artist cried.

The banker frowned. "What about the risk?"

The engineer shrugged. "As long each of them thinks I'm with the other I can go to the lab and get something done."

* * *

As a confessed engineer, you may think I lack not only the credentials but even the aptitude to discuss romance. You may be right, at least in terms of how we commonly approach the topic, but even romance has structural principles.

RESPECT

For a romance to succeed the hero and the heroine—even if they spar—must never lose each other's respect: they must never lose sight of the lovable in the other.

Consider **Pride and Prejudice**: Darcy might be haughty and disdainful, but he's always respectable. Some of that is simply a consequence of his station in the social structure, but the greater part of his respectability flows from the way he navigates his circumstances. Even when he's working against Elizabeth by undermining Jane's relationship with Bingley he does so for respectable reasons (i.e., concern for his friend's welfare).

Here are some corollaries about the foundation of a romance:

- Never make either of your protagonists unlikable. The hero has to be someone the heroine can look up to. The heroine must be someone the hero can trust.

- Never make your protagonists look stupid. The hero and heroine can be at odds, but they must never undermine each other; they must retain an underlying core of admirability—something redeeming about them—that the other can see.

EACH PARTNER COMPLETES THE OTHER

I don't know if it's a trend—or simply something I never noticed before—but of late I've seen a number of explicitly complementary Halloween costumes for couples: you and your partner can, for example, dress as a plug and socket or a key and a lock.

After you're done giggling (or, with your best Queen Victoria impression, being, "Not amused,") at the sexual innuendo, remember that there was a time before the triumph of interchangeable parts when only one key fit a given lock.

Mutual respect is the structural foundation of a romance. Respect is necessary but not sufficient to explain why a couple came together. Each partner likely respects several potential mates so there must be something more that brings two people together.

In a good romance, each partner fulfills a need in the other: they complete each other.

You might be tempted to either get sappy about the one key to someone's heart or to wax rhapsodic about soul-mates. What we're really talking about is a structural completion: each partner is a better person or more fully alive when they are with the other.

More than simply the act of falling in love, romance is about the possibilities that spring into existence when two people come together to create a whole that is greater than the sum of its parts.

THE JOURNEY TOWARD EACH OTHER

At the end of **When Harry Met Sally...**, the titular couple appear in the pseudo-documentary that punctuates transition points in the movie in which various couples tell how they came together:

Harry: The third time we met, we became friends.

Sally: We were friends for a long time.
Harry: And then we weren't.
Sally: And then we fell in love.

That, in a nutshell, is the arc of a classic romance. More formally, a classic romance has three phases:

- **The Meeting**—this is as important as setting up the quest; here the reader decides whether it's worth the time to follow the story. The meeting leaves the reader wondering, "How in the world are they ever going to overcome their problems and get together?"

- **The Courtship**—the ups and downs as the couple attempts to come together. If you have a conflict between the hero and the heroine that could be resolved if they had a five-minute conversation, you don't have enough of a conflict to carry the story.

- **The Happily-ever-after**—in terms of overall structure, if the story doesn't end with the couple together in a committed relationship, it's not a classic romance. As romantic as portions of Romeo and Juliet may be, the story is, in fact, a tragedy.

A romance is analogous to a hero's journey at several levels.

First, they are both fundamentally about journeys that cross the space separating a problem and its resolution. But where a quest involves crossing a physical space, a romance is about crossing social and emotional space. Also, at a fairly abstract level, both kinds of journeys involve separation (the hero from the village he's trying to save, the couple from each other) and eventual reunion, but a quest has a single character arc where a romance has two.

Second, both kinds of stories must have several try/fail cycles. Just as a hero who saves the village with a fifteen-minute trip to the convenience store isn't much of a hero, a couple who meet and head right to the wedding chapel doesn't provide much romance. Such things, of course, do happen in the real world, but as narratives they're barely worthy of a short story.

Try/fail cycles demonstrate that the stakes are far greater than the protagonists (and the reader) imagined. The hero's first attempt to right the wrong usually results in them getting knocked down, perhaps almost killed. Similarly, the couple's first meeting should show as many or more reasons why they'll never get together as why they might. The failure, however, is never complete and shows that the hoped-for outcome is still possible.

But there's more going on in the try/fail cycles of a romance than, "Could it work? No. Could it work? No. Could it work? Yes." The key difference is that a romance follows the trajectories of two people who must not only find each other, they must find in the other someone they respect and who completes them. In both **Pride and Prejudice** and **Jane Eyre**, the heroines had to reject the first offer of marriage because the resulting union would have been dangerously unbalanced.

The couple's journey together is the substance of the second phase (the courtship) in a classic romance. There are, of course, more dimensions to an actual romance, but if you can show, through try/fail cycles, how the two people develop a balanced partnership, without ever losing respect for each other, until they reach the point where they can see how they complete each other, your romance will have a high degree of verisimilitude.

QUEST AND ROMANCE: OIL AND WATER?

At a conference presentation on romance, the speaker asked which male character in the original **Star Wars** trilogy (episodes IV – VI for you youngsters) was most romantic. The audience voted overwhelmingly for Han Solo.

Why not Luke? It is, after all, the story of how he becomes a hero.

The answer is in the verb near the end of the previous sentence: becomes.

What is Han? Easy: he's a rogue and space pirate (and some of you might insist on adding the qualifier, "devilishly handsome").

What is Luke? It depends on when you ask. At different times he is a farm boy, an orphan, an apprentice, a pilot, a soldier, a student, a son, a Jedi, a brother, and a savior. All of these are aspects of Luke becoming a hero—which is as it should be because the hero's journey is fundamentally about a character's transformation.

Now think about the classic romance pattern: the romantic lead is often well-established in some fashion. For example, we meet Mr. Darcy when he's the master of Pemberly, not as the callow youth being sent off to school for the first time. Han Solo has the Millennium Falcon and has made a place (albeit a tenuous one) for himself in the galaxy. As clichéd as it sounds now, there was a time when the guy in high school with the car got more attention from the girls because it was evidence he had the wherewithal to acquire and operate an expensive piece of machinery.

Here's the key point: you can't have a classic romance while the hero and/or heroine are transforming themselves from debatable youths to wiser, tested, and fundamentally more admirable people. For example, in Lloyd Alexander's **Chronicles of Prydain**, it is clear Taran and Eilonwy are fond of each other in the first book, but their romance doesn't blossom until the final volume. In the intervening books, they both go through one or more transforming journeys largely on their own.

This, of course, isn't an argument that you can't have a classic romance in high school. And heaven knows real life is a perplexing muddle of being and becoming. But in terms of structure, where a hero's journey is as much about becoming an individual who can stand on his or her own as it is about the external threat, a classic romance is about distinct individuals becoming a couple.

They are fundamentally different kinds of stories.

NATURAL ROMANCE

How do you make a romance feel natural?

Within the overall qualification of Maslow's hierarchy of needs (i.e., a couple probably won't worry about working out the nuances of their relationship if they're starving), romance can blossom anywhere. Even though everyone laughs, the moment in **The Empire Strikes Back** right before Han is frozen in carbonite when Leia professes her love and Han says, "I know," is deeply romantic if you remember how nervous they (and the audience) are about Han's fate.

On the other hand, the accoutrements of romance—food, wine, music, low lights—are more likely to produce unnatural romance, where the couple play their parts but their hearts aren't in it because, at best, they are in love with being in love.

Like the force, natural romance flows from the characters, not from the setting.

Natural romance involves people with flaws. Perfect people are as unnatural as a perfectly romantic setting. But to be natural, the flaws must be neither superficial nor pathological.

If the romance is a subplot, it needs to have bearing on the story. Romance isn't a condiment that you can add to a story to spice it up. Use sex for that—everyone else does—but don't mistake sex for romance.

Natural romance is a growing, dynamic thing. It's not an all or nothing affair. While there are certainly people who are like volatile chemicals together, swinging between the extremes of love and hate because of the intensity of their passions, very few of those couples achieve the happily-ever-after of a stable, committed relationship. That's not to say couples developing a natural romance won't have their ups and downs, but that their overall trajectory is to grow closer over time.

BIOLOGY, GENDER, AND CHARACTER

Our biological imperative to mate could be satisfied with the first healthy, willing, and able member of the opposite sex we find. Unlike many mammals that breed when the female is in estrus (heat), that's not how we work. Because sexually mature members of our species can breed at any time, the complex process by which we select a partner from among available mates is informed by concerns that span Maslow's hierarchy from basic sexual drives through family, culture, and society, to abstract notions of beauty, love, and truth. The way your characters approach romance speaks volumes about them.

There are important, if sometimes subtle differences between the genders. A crucial part of coming together is learning to live with someone who can at times make you doubt the fact that you are members of the same species. Some say that where men are compartmentalized, women relate everything to everything else, creating emotional ties between things that men would never recognize as related. The differences are important because in them the couple find strengths to complement each other's weaknesses. If your hero and heroine think and act exactly alike, you don't have a romance you have a narcissistic duet.

RHYME AND REASON

The bottom line is that natural romance has rhyme and reason. The rhythm may not be apparent to the characters (or the readers) in the midst of the process, but even in the moments that seem most irrational, it's still there. As with many other aspects, a romance has verisimilitude when the reader believes there are reasons for what's happening.

A natural romance is a character-driven mating dance, with tension and chemistry as the couple get to know each other and learn how to live together.

A TIME AND A PLACE

Given the title, you may expect curmudgeonly comments along the lines of, "Get a room!" but what I really want to talk about is food poisoning.

Once, in a conversation with my brother-in-law, he

mentioned that he'd suffered through a bout of food poisoning.

I asked how he knew it was food poisoning.

"You know sometimes you're sick enough that you're afraid you might die?" he said. "With food poisoning you're sick enough that you're afraid you might live!"

I know it's not a pleasant topic. I mention it, however, because when my turn came to be ill enough to fear that I might live I didn't give a single thought to romance.

In a computer simulation of simple organisms, the creatures moved through their environment searching for food and could reproduce only after they had accumulated enough excess energy. Of course, movement burned energy and resources weren't evenly distributed, so the organisms had to develop search strategies to find enough food without travelling too far to be able to reproduce. As abstract as that simulation was, it captured an important element of natural romance: because it takes effort above and beyond what is required to simply survive, there's a time and a place for it.

Love and intimacy don't register until the third tier of the Maslow Hierarchy of Needs. Sex, however, figures prominently among the physiological needs in the first tier. That gap illustrates the difference between reproduction as a biological imperative and romance. Indeed, natural romance is as much about the fourth tier—esteem: respect of others and respect by others—as it is about the third. And true love, in a partnership where you're a genuinely better person because of the other, moves you toward the pinnacle of the pyramid.

This hierarchy also shows why romance occurs only after people have established themselves as competent, viable individuals (i.e., they have learned how to satisfy their needs on at least the first two tiers).

In addition to these structural needs, there are corresponding needs for time and a place in the social and cultural dimensions. For example, most societies frown on excessive displays of affection in public spheres. Because we are social creatures, finding a partner who knows how to behave appropriately is as important as a partner who is healthy and knows how to acquire and manage the resources that satisfy our physiological and safety needs. (So I suppose I really have come full circle back to, "Get a room!")

More to the point, unless your story is specifically about people living way outside social and psychological norms, natural romance is much more about patience and discretion than passion and erratic behavior.

WORKING TOGETHER

During an especially stressful time in the series **Babylon 5**, when the titular space station was cut off from Earth by a civil war, a visiting minister advised the captain to find someone with whom he could share his burdens:

"You know, before I got married, Emily used to come by sometimes and help me clean out my apartment. Well, I asked her, "How come you're so eager to help me clean up my place when your place is just as bad? She said, "Because cleaning up your place helps me to forget what a mess I made of mine. And when I sweep my floor, all I've done is sweep my floor. But when I help you clean up your place, I am helping you." Of course, the way I lived back then sometimes the mess was too much for both of us, but ... it sure was nice to have the company."

Natural romances are also long-form stories. There are a lot of hours to pass when you're spending your lives together and in the grand sweep of time, most of those hours will be spent on romantic things like sleeping and working.

"Sleeping and working," you may object, "are hardly romantic."

But if you enjoy the company and appreciate the help, just about anything can contribute to your romance when you're working together. When we were dating, I once took my wife to help me milk a cow. My sisters were appalled that I called it a date, but we had a lovely time—and it was the beginning of many such lovely times.

A number of species have mating dances, in which the partners synchronize their movements as they draw closer together. In many cases, the dance displays the health and vigor of the individuals and proves their suitability as a mate. We are, of course, much more sophisticated than the creatures with which we share the planet and yet romance can be seen as a mating dance that spans dimensions from the physiological to the social. Our goal in each of those dimensions is to find out if we can work together because that's one of the main ways couples complete each other.

The verisimilitude of your romance will suffer if your couple does nothing except share candle-lit suppers and passionate evenings. In contrast, natural romances are often kindled between people who have done something difficult together: the shared experience provides strong evidence that they can work together. So when you're stocking up to provision your romance, don't forget the elbow-grease.

CHAPTER 26.

THE GRAND UNIFICATION OF PLOT AND CHARACTER

You could certainly argue that the hero's journey is about plot because the key beats involve external action. Similarly, the arc of the virgin's promise is about character because the key beats are internal. But there's also a case to be made that the hero's journey is, in the deepest sense, about the development of the hero's character. And, because the virgin's promise is about the process by which she claims a place in her world instead of simply submitting to the wishes and expectations of others, her story is fundamentally about taking action.

Carrie Vaugh said:

> "Plot and character are the same thing. A story's actions should arise out of the decisions and reactions those particular characters make. Different characters would drive the story in a different direction.... Changing the characters, the kinds of people they are, would change the story. If the events of a story would happen no matter who the characters are ... why should I want to read about them?" [7]

We're often told to raise the stakes in our stories: why have the bad guy threaten to blow up a city block when he could blow up the entire city! But there are diminishing returns as you continue to raise the stakes. The terrorists are about to detonate a home-made nuclear device that will kill a million people. That's frightening. Now we raise the stakes by adding a nuclear scientist to the terrorist line up who knows how to make a better bomb, one that can kill ten million people. Is that ten times as frightening?

The scope of what's at stake is at best secondary to the significance of what's at stake. That's why a quiet book about someone's heart being broken by an untimely death will elicit more tears than a shoot-em-up where bodies fall faster than autumn leaves.

I'm sure you've heard literary fiction characterized as character-drive in contrast to plot-driven commercial fiction. But the deeper truth is that good stories, regardless of the genre, are about things that matter.

And how do we know what matters?

Because someone cares about it.

Significance is a fascinating concept because it is not an objective property. Significance only exists because we attribute it. Washington, D.C., sits on a patch of ground that was utterly insignificant until George Washington convinced people it should be the capital. Once a few people cared about it, a great many others came to care about it too.

This leads us to a grand unification theory: character and plot are the internal and external aspects of a deeper, underlying unity flowing from the fact that meaningful stories are about the people and things that matter to the people in the stories that matter to us.

ACKNOWLEDGEMENTS

This series of writing guides grew out of a collection of posts on my blog, **The Laws of Making**, representing a conversation of sorts with the following people, each of whom helped me sharpen my thinking about writing and the writing life:

Podcasts: Sarah Eden, Patrick Hester, Marion Jensen, Mary Robinette Kowal, Mur Lafferty, L.E. Modesitt, Brandon Sanderson, Howard Tayler, Dan Wells, Robinson Wells.

Conference Panels and Presentations: John Brown, Jaleta Clegg, James Dashner, Bree Despain, Jessica Day George, Laura Hickman, Tracy Hickman, Jeanette Ingold, Clint Johnson, Lynn Kurland, Scott Livingston, Leslie Muir Lytle, Brandon Mull, Sheila Nelson, Janette Rallison, Sandra Tayler, Joanna Volpe, Stacy Whitman, Julie Wright.

Posts: Brunonia Barry, Holly Black, Livia Blackburn, Michael Bourret, Sarah Callender, Adam Carolla, Toni McGee Causey, Eric Cummings, Julie Danes, Stephanie DeVita, Anne Gallagher, Janet Grant, Elizabeth Gumport, Meghan Cox Gurdon, P.J. Hoover, Austin Kleon, Stina Linderblatt, Annette Lyons, Juliet Marillier, Bob Mayer,

Jael McHenry, Heather Moore, Aprilynne Pike, Simon Pulman, Erin Reel, Holly Root, Kristine Kathryn Rusch, Jon Sternfeld, Rebecca Talley, Heidi M. Thomas, Carrie Vaugh, John Vorhaus, Chuck Wendig, Scott Westerfeld, Zoe Winters, Julie Wright, Howard Yoon, Sara Zarr.

Blogs: Nathan Bransford, Jessica Faust, Rachelle Gardner, Jeff Hirsch, Mary Kole, Kristin Nelson, Kate Testerman, Becca Wilhite.

Thank you.

NOTES

I've provided the following links for those who would like further information about sources of quotes and other selected topics. Some of the links go to Amazon because there are no better sources of information. I've included those links for your convenience. They are not affiliate links and I receive no benefit if you make a purchase.

NOTES FOR STORY THEORY

CHAPTER 2: STORIES ARE MODELS

[1] Warren G. Bennis and James O'Toole, "How Business Schools Lost Their Way," **Harvard Business Review**, May 2005.

[2] See the Wikipedia article on Checkov's Gun: http://en.wikipedia.org/wiki/Chekhov%27s_gun

[3] Matthew Frederick, **101 Things I Learned in Architecture School**, MIT Press, 2007. [See Amazon.] Toni McGee Causey quoted Matthew Frederick in a post on the **Murderati** blog that expands on the implications of positive and negative spaces for writers. See: http://www.murderati.com/positive-and-negative-spaces/

CHAPTER 4: THREE IS A MAGIC NUMBER

[4] The **Star Trek Roleplaying Game Narrator's Guide** appears to be out of print, but some information is available at Amazon.

[5] Justine Musk shared her observations about the importance of the middle in a 2011 post on her blog. See: http://www.tribalwriter.com/2011/05/06/the-secrets-and-revelations-of-a-powerful-middle-act/

[6] Schoolhouse Rock was broadcast during Saturday morning children's programming by the ABC network during 1973-1985 and 1993-1999. See the Wikipedia article for an overview: http://en.wikipedia.org/wiki/Schoolhouse_Rock!

CHAPTER 5: COMPLEX STORIES ARE FRACTAL

[7] For an introductory discussion of algorithms to simulate flocking behavior, see the Wikipedia article: http://en.wikipedia.org/wiki/Flocking_%28behavior%29

CHAPTER 6: STORY DRIVERS

[8] The term, "red shirt," comes from **Star Trek**, where nameless security people in red shirts expired so often that the uniform became synonymous with characters that die shortly after you get to know them. See the Wikipedia article on red shirts: http://en.wikipedia.org/wiki/Redshirt_(character)

A, "Mary Sue," character is usually too-good to be true, embodying skills and characteristics the author wishes he or she possessed. See the Wikipedia article on Mary Sue characters: http://en.wikipedia.org/wiki/Mary_Sue

[9] See the Wikipedia article for an overview of the film, **Willow**, at: http://en.wikipedia.org/wiki/Willow_(film)

CHAPTER 7: CONFLICT

[10] You can read the Monty Python, "Self-defense Against Fresh Fruit," sketch at: http://www.montypython.net/scripts/fruit.php

[11] *La guerra del fútbol*, or Soccer War, between Honduras and El Savador in 1969 is well-summarized in a Wikipedia article. See: http://en.wikipedia.org/wiki/Football_War

CHAPTER 8: THE ART OF THE LONG FORM

[12] Donald Maass discussed the elements of a fully-developed premise in a 2012 post at **Writer Unboxed**. See: http://writerunboxed.com/2012/04/04/the-good-seed/

[13] See the Wikipedia article on variation as a formal musical technique: http://en.wikipedia.org/wiki/Variation_%28music%29

CHAPTER 9: EDITING AND REVISIONS

[14] Jael McHenry talked about the two senses of the word compromise in a post at **Writer Unboxed**. See: http://writerunboxed.com/2011/02/07/revise-without-compromise/

[15] Jessica Faust discussed responding to agents too quickly in a post on her blog. See: http://bookendslitagency.blogspot.com/2011/01/revisions-from-agent.html

NOTES FOR VERISIMILITUDE

CHAPTER 1: THE APPEARANCE OF TRUTH

[1] **The Last Battle** is the final book in C.S. Lewis's series, **The Chronicles of Narnia**. See Wikipedia for a synopsis: http://en.wikipedia.org/wiki/The_Last_Battle

CHAPTER 2: A READERS' BILL OF RIGHTS

[2] Mark Twain set down his rules for writing as part of an essay on *Fenimore Cooper's Literary Offenses*. The good folk at PBS have made the entire essay available. See: http://www.pbs.org/marktwain/learnmore/writings_fenimore.html

[3] Kurt Vonnegut, **Bagombo Snuff Box: Uncollected Short Fiction,** G.P. Putnam's Sons, 1999, pp. 9-10. Vonnegut's eight rules are listed, along with a great deal of information about the author on his Wikipedia page. See: http://en.wikipedia.org/wiki/Kurt_Vonnegut#Self-assessment

CHAPTER 3: SOMETHING TO THINK ABOUT

[4] John Sternfeld made his comments about engaged readers in a post at **Writer's Digest**. See: http://www.writersdigest.com/editor-blogs/guide-to-literary-agents/agent-jon-sternfeld-on-engaging-your-audience

CHAPTER 5: COMPETENT WORDSMITHING

[5] Eric Cummings discussed saying what you mean in a 2009 post on the **Write to Done** blog. See:

http://writetodone.com/2009/12/17/the-golden-rule-of-writing/

[6] Sol Stein's, **Stein on Writing**, published in 2000 continues to sell well because it is filled with good advice. You can take a look at it on Amazon.

CHAPTER 7: MAKE SURE THE NUMBERS ADD UP

[7] See Wikipedia to learn more about **Plan 9 from Outer Space**, if you dare, at: http://en.wikipedia.org/wiki/Plan_9_from_Outer_Space

[8] See Wikipedia for an overview of Aprilynne Pike's novel, **Wings**: http://en.wikipedia.org/wiki/Wings_(Pike_novel)

CHAPTER 8: GETTING THINGS RIGHT

[9] See the Wikipedia article on **The Republic**, by Plato, at: http://en.wikipedia.org/wiki/The_Republic_(Plato)

[10] See Wikipedia for an overview of Jared Diamond's book, **Collapse**, at: http://en.wikipedia.org/wiki/Collapse:_How_Societies_Choose_to_Fail_or_Succeed

CHAPTER 9: WRITING INTENTIONALLY

[11] Nathan Bransford's list of things you should know before you write a novel comes from a 2010 post on his blog. See: http://blog.nathanbransford.com/2010/08/how-to-write-novel.html

[12] There's a fascinating essay by J. Clements at the **ARMA** website about the myths and realities of medieval swords. See: http://www.thearma.org/essays/weights.htm

NOTES FOR CHARACTER AND ARCHETYPE

CHAPTER 2: NATURAL CHARACTERIZATION

[1] Orson Scott Card's, **Characters and Viewpoint** is probably the best place to go to continue your study of character and characterization. See Amazon.

CHAPTER 3: CHARACTER DYNAMICS

[2] For an introduction to Mazlow and his hierarchy, see the Wikipedia article at: http://en.wikipedia.org/wiki/Maslow's_hierarchy_of_needs

CHAPTER 4: THE HERO'S JOURNEY

[3] See Wikipedia for a summary of Joseph Campbell and his work at: http://en.wikipedia.org/wiki/Joseph_Campbell.

[4] Wikipedia also has a good summary of Campbell's monomyth, or the hero's journey. See: http://en.wikipedia.org/wiki/Monomyth

[5] Christopher Vogler's, **The Writer's Journey**, though aimed at screenwriters, is an excellent study of the mythic structure of the hero's journey. You can find it at Amazon. See Wikipedia for a summary of Vogler's book: http://en.wikipedia.org/wiki/The_Writer%27s_Journey:_Mythic_Structure_for_Writers

CHAPTER 5: THE VIRGIN'S PROMISE

[6] My primary source and inspiration is Kim Hudson's, **The Virgin's Promise**, which expands on Vogler's work (among others) and develops a parallel structure for stories of self-fulfillment. Do yourself a favor and get a copy. See Amazon.

CHAPTER 7: THE GRAND UNIFICATION OF PLOT AND CHARACTER

[7] Carrie Vaugh discussed the unification of plot and character in a post at **Writer's Digest**. See: http://www.writersdigest.com/editor-blogs/guide-to-literary-agents/7-things-ive-learned-so-far-by-carrie-vaughn

Made in the USA
San Bernardino, CA
20 April 2018